Table of Contents

Rainstorm®

Copyright © 2020 Kidsbooks, LLC
All rights reserved
Rainstorm Publishing is an imprint
and a trademark of Kidsbooks®, LLC
Kidsbooks Publishing
3535 West Peterson Avenue
Chicago, IL 60659
Printed in China
www.kidsbookspublishing.com

Learn how to **write** the letter A a
by **tracing** the outlines.

A Alligator

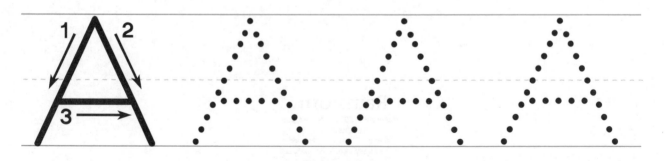

a alligator

B

Learn how to **write** the letter Bb
by **tracing** the outlines.

Bear

1
2
3

B B B B B

b bear

1
2

C

Learn how to **write** the letter Cc
by **tracing** the outlines.

C Cow

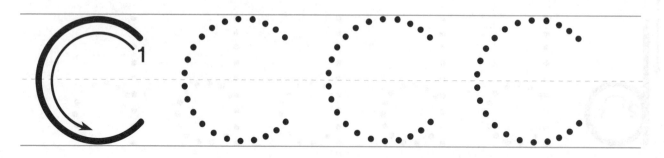

C cow

D

Learn how to **write** the letter Dd
by **tracing** the outlines.

D Duck

d duck

E

Learn how to **write** the letter E e
by **tracing** the outlines.

E Elephant

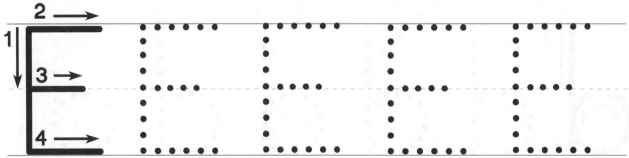

e elephant

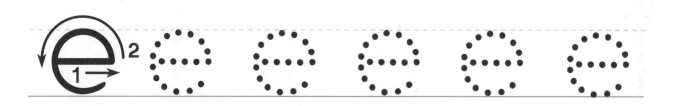

F

Learn how to **write** the letter F f
by **tracing** the outlines.

Frog

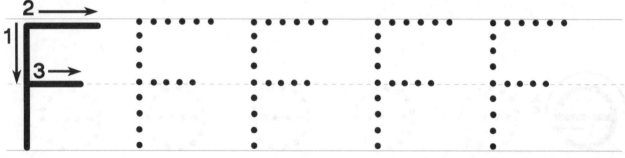

f frog

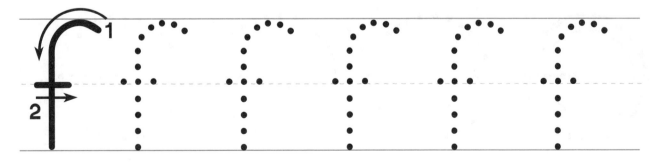

G

Learn how to **write** the letter Gg
by **tracing** the outlines.

Giraffe

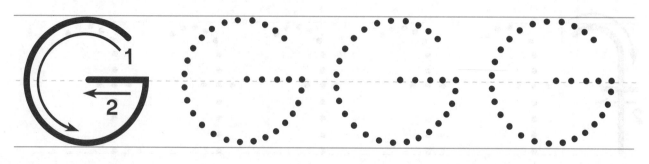

g giraffe

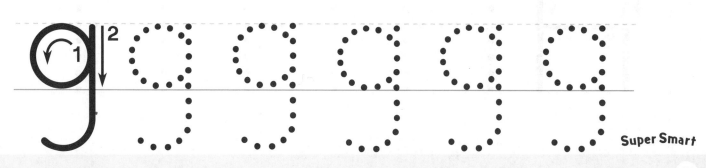

H

Learn how to **write** the letter Hh
by **tracing** the outlines.

H Horse

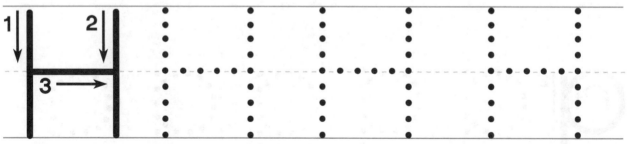

h horse

I

Learn how to **write** the letter Ii
by **tracing** the outlines.

Iguana

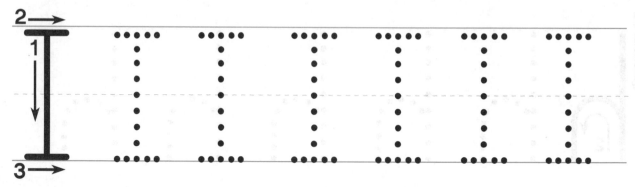

I iguana

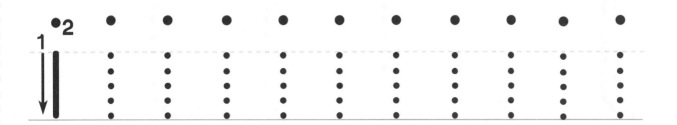

J

Learn how to **write** the letter J j
by **tracing** the outlines.

J Jaguar

2 →

1

J J J J J

j jaguar

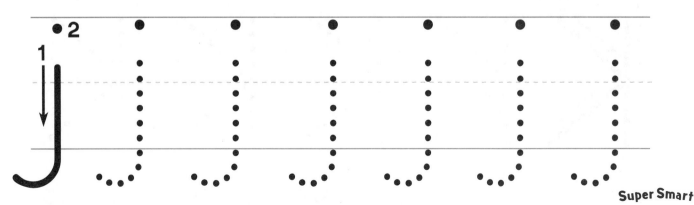

K

Learn how to **write** the letter K k
by **tracing** the outlines.

K Kangaroo

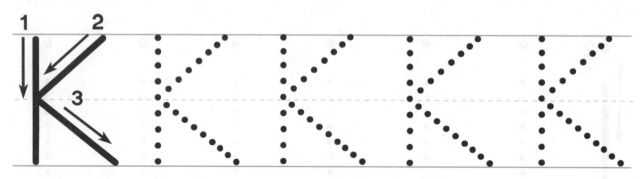

k kangaroo

L

Learn how to **write** the letter L l
by **tracing** the outlines.

Lion

1
2

l lion

1

M

Learn how to **write** the letter M m
by **tracing** the outlines.

Moose

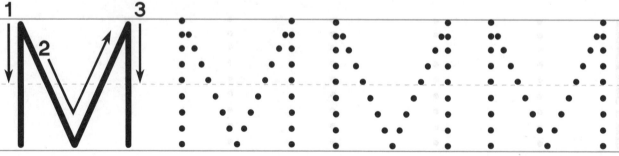

m moose

N

Learn how to **write** the letter N n
by **tracing** the outlines.

Nuthatch

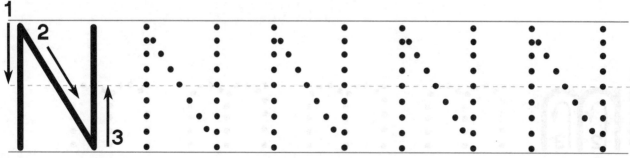

n nuthatch

Learn how to **write** the letter O o
by **tracing** the outlines.

Owl

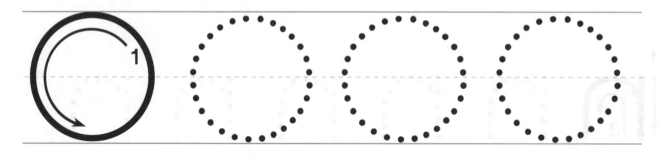

O owl

P

Learn how to **write** the letter P p
by **tracing** the outlines.

P Penguin

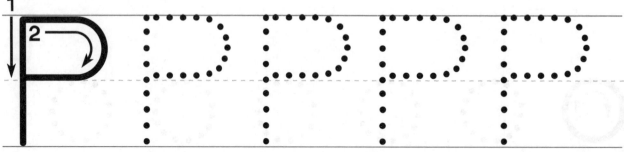

p penguin

Learn how to **write** the letter Qq
by **tracing** the outlines.

Q Quail

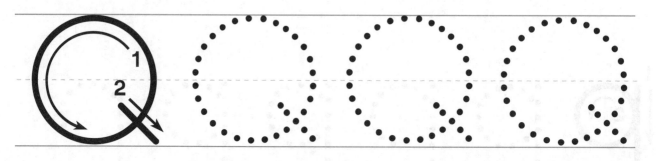

q quail

q

R

Learn how to **write** the letter Rr
by **tracing** the outlines.

R Raccoon

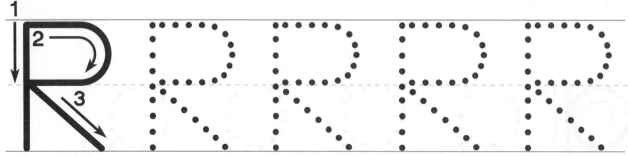

r raccoon

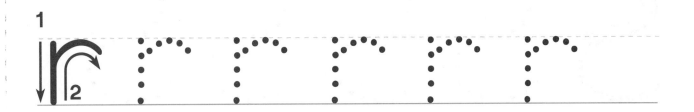

S

Learn how to **write** the letter Ss
by **tracing** the outlines.

Seahorse

S

S seahorse

S¹ S S S S S

T

Learn how to **write** the letter T t
by **tracing** the outlines.

T Turtle

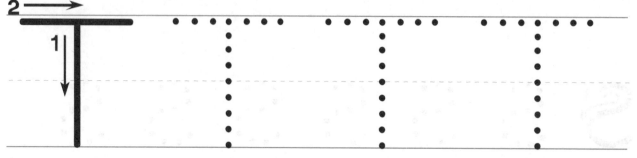

t turtle

U

Learn how to **write** the letter Uu
by **tracing** the outlines.

Urial

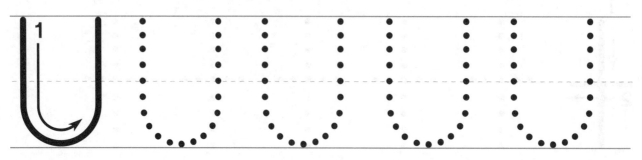

U urial

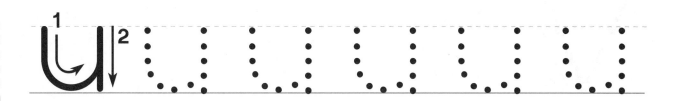

Learn how to **write** the letter V v
by **tracing** the outlines.

V Vole

V vole

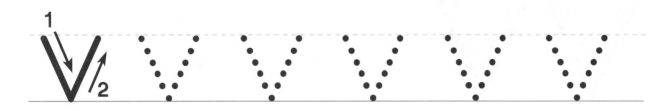

W

Learn how to **write** the letter W w
by **tracing** the outlines.

Whale

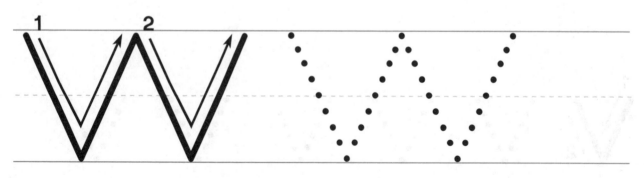

W whale

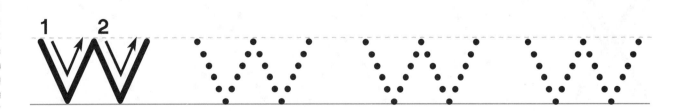

X

Learn how to **write** the letter X x by **tracing** the outlines.

X-ray Fish

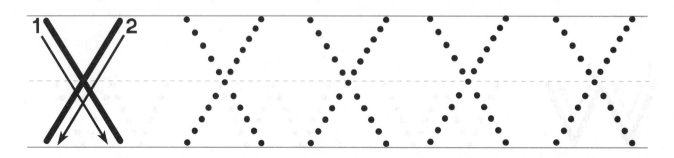

X x-ray fish

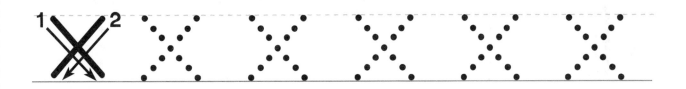

Learn how to **write** the letter Y y
by **tracing** the outlines.

Y Yak

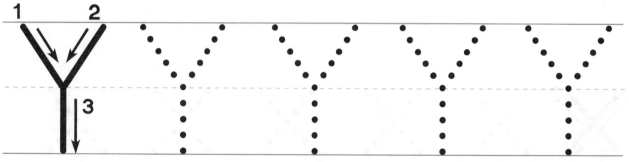

Y yak

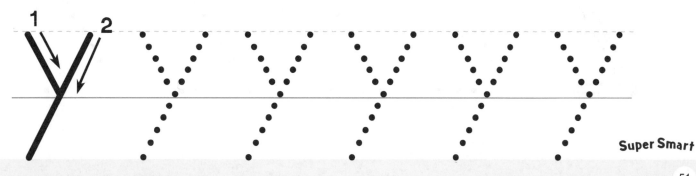

Z

Learn how to **write** the letter Z z
by **tracing** the outlines.

Z Zebra

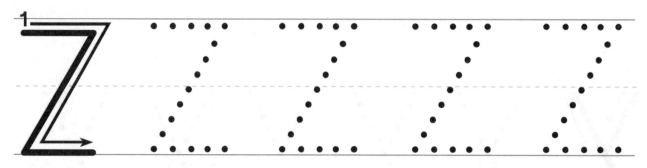

Z zebra

Z z z z z

Trace the Uppercase Alphabet

Trace the dotted lines to write the letters of the alphabet.

Trace the Lowercase Alphabet

Trace the dotted lines to write the letters of the alphabet.

a b c d e

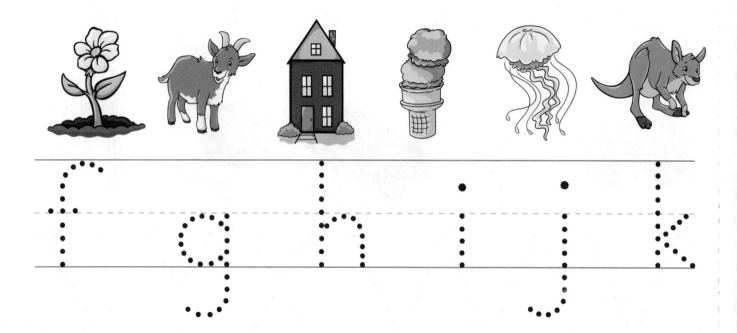

f g h i j k

Which Doesn't Rhyme?

In each group of pictures one picture doesn't rhyme with the others. **Cross out** the non-rhyming word.

Jungle Stomp

Connect the dots from A – N to discover the hidden picture. Then **color** it!

A B C D E F G H I J K L M N

Hermit Crab

Connect the dots from O – Z to discover the hidden picture. Then **color** it!

O P Q R S T U V W X Y Z

Fridge Letters

Circle the letter magnets that are lowercase.

Underwater Letters

Find the nine hidden letters in the picture and **circle** them.

a e f l m o p s u

Write Your Name!

Which letters do you use to spell your name?
Practice **writing** your name in the spaces below.

A B C D E F G H I J K L M

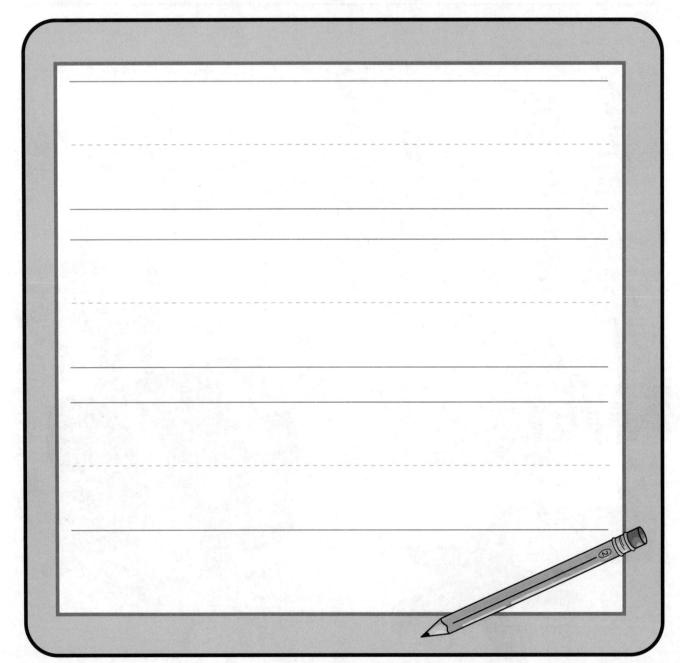

N O P Q R S T U V W X Y Z

Animal Words

Practice **tracing** these words.

dog

fish

cat

bird

Crossword Color

Color the picture with red and blue. Then **write** the name of each color in the crossword.

The fire hydrant is ⬚.

The water is .

Rhyming Pairs

Draw a line to connect each rhyming pair.

Four in a Row

Find and **circle** four items in a row that begin with each letter below.

Four in a Row

Find and **circle** four items in a row that begin with each letter below.

Missing Letters

Some of the letters are missing in the alphabet. See if you can **fill them in**!

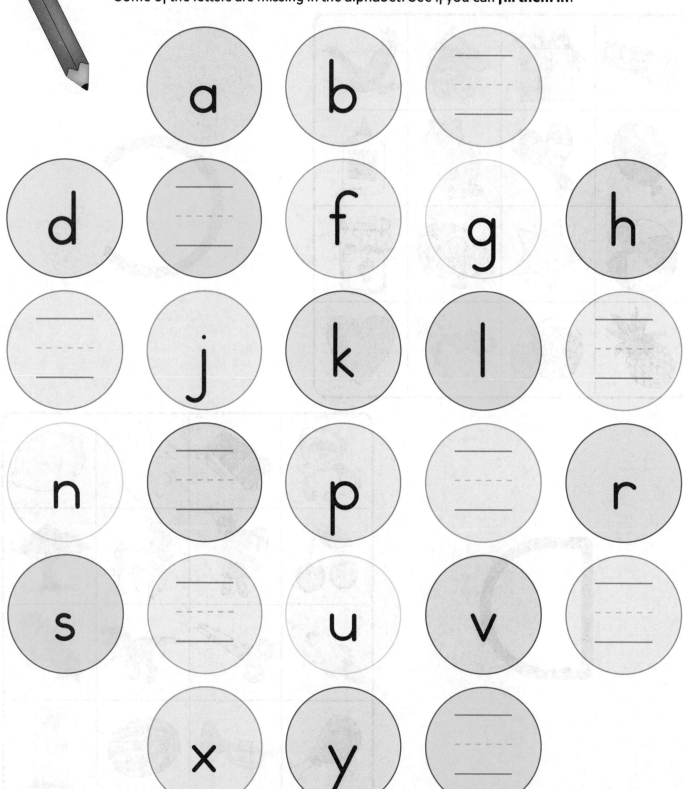

a   b   ___

d   ___   f   g   h

___   j   k   l   ___

n   ___   p   ___   r

s   ___   u   v   ___

x   y   ___

Matching Letters

Circle the matching lowercase letter for each uppercase letter.

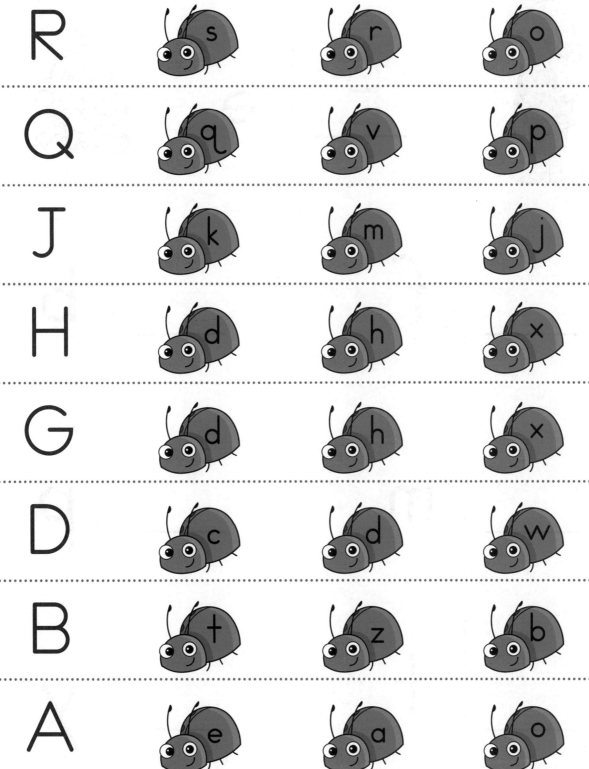

Which is the Uppercase?

Write the matching lowercase letter for each uppercase letter.

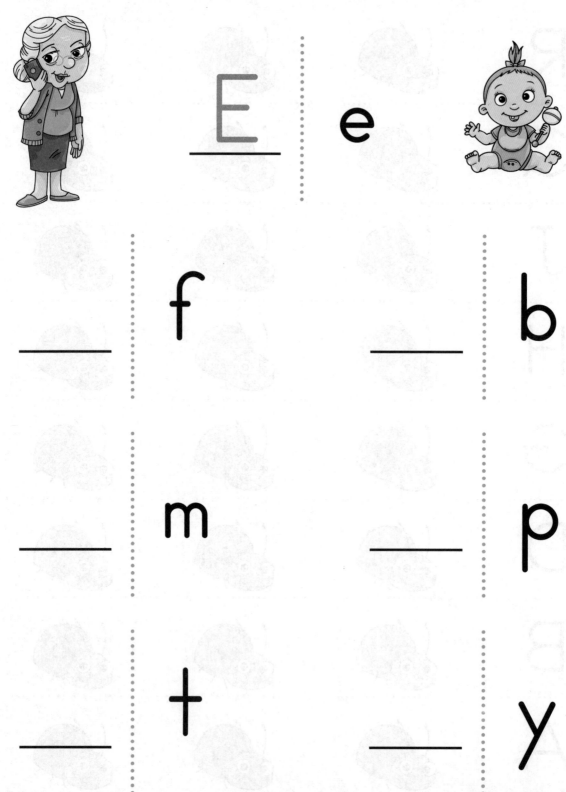

E ___ | e

___ | f ___ | b

___ | m ___ | p

___ | t ___ | y

Starting Letter

Circle the letter each of the images below begins with.

c

w

s

f

y

p

g

t

r

x

h

b

Letter Maze

Trace the path to lead one animal to the other.
Can you **find** the hidden letter inside each maze?

Letter Maze

Trace the path to lead one animal to the other.
Can you **find** the hidden letter inside each maze?

Space Travel

Trace the loops, zigs, and zags of these rockets and astronauts.

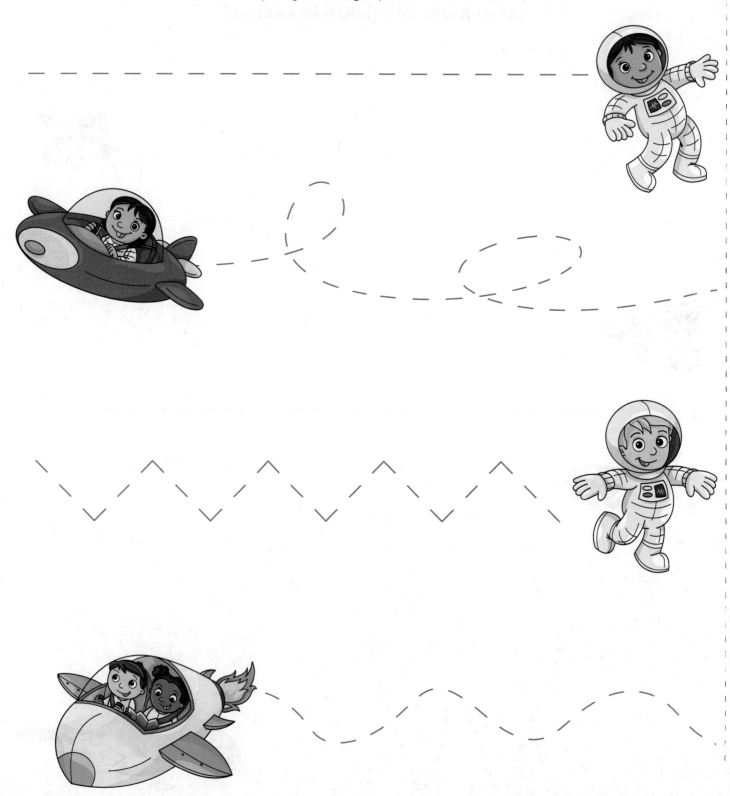

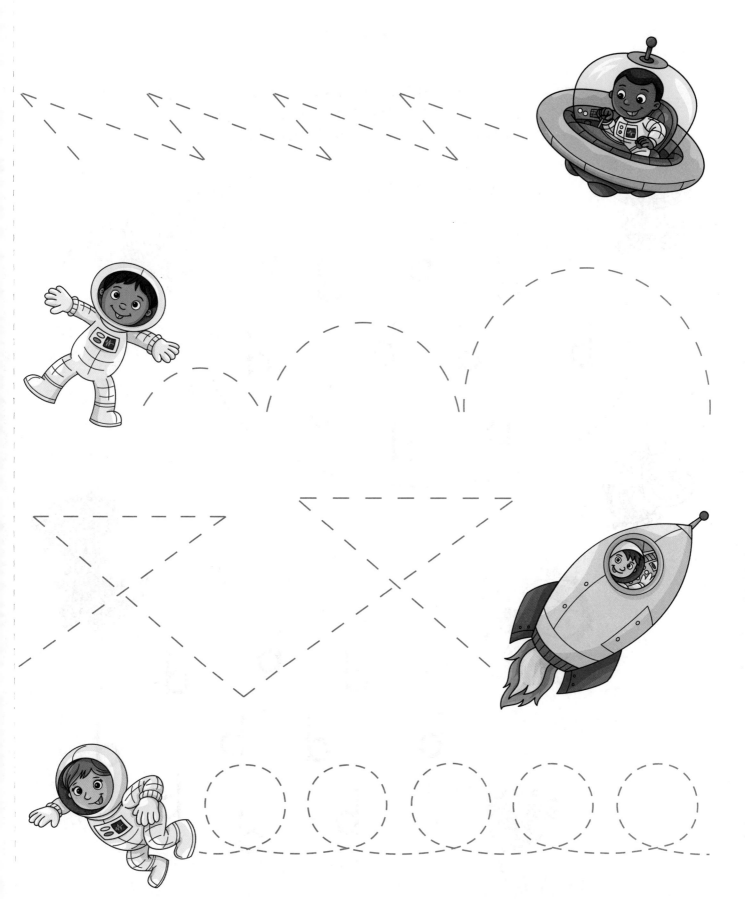

b or d?

Lowercase b's and d's look very similar.
One has the circle on the left, and one on the right.
Follow the instructions below to **circle** either the b's or d's.

Circle the b's.

Circle the d's.

q or p?

Lowercase q's and p's look very similar.
One has the circle on the left, and one on the right. Q's have a little tail on the bottom.
Follow the instructions below to **circle** either the q's or p's.

Circle the q's.

p q p
q p q q
p q p

Circle the p's.

p q p
q p q q
p q p

First Sounds

For each of the animals below, **say** their name and **listen** to the first sound you hear.
Then **draw** a line between the letter and the picture that starts with the matching sound.

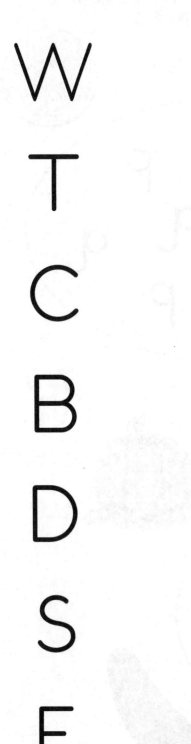

First Letter

Use the pictures to help you **fill in** the missing first letter in the words below.

n • k • p • a • b • f • t

 = __ o x

 = __ e y

 = __ p p l e

 = __ e s t

= __ r e e

 = __ a g

 = __ i e

Snail Alphabet

Help the snails get to their shells by **drawing** a line between
matching uppercase and lowercase letters.

First Words

Draw a line to connect each image with its matching word.

tree

mug

dog

hat

car

cat

fish

bed

sock

frog

bath

bird

Which Word Doesn't Belong?

Cross out the picture that doesn't begin with the same letter as the others in each row.

cat   car   dog   cake

hat   bird   boy   bear

fire   spider   fish   frog

turtle   train   tiger   starfish

moon   monkey   net   mouse

Sand Trace

Trace these beach words in the sandy space below.

sand

hat

sun

crab

boat

shell

sea

WXYZ

For each letter below, **circle** the picture that begins with that letter.

W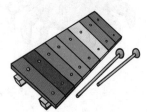

X

Y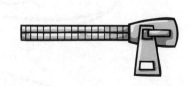

Z

Rhyming Pairs

Draw a line to connect each rhyming pair.

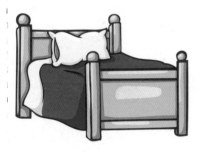

Super Smart

Counting Syllables

For each picture below, **say** the word and **circle** the dots to show how many syllables they have.

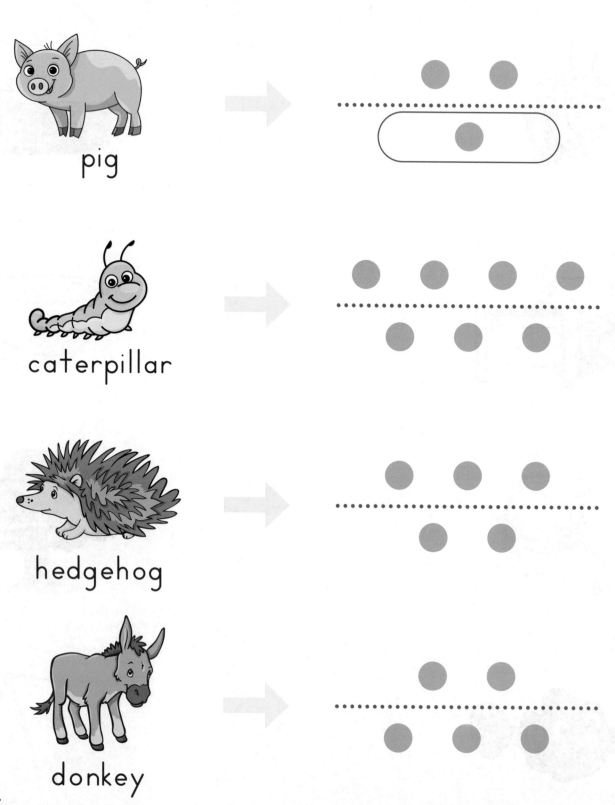

pig

caterpillar

hedgehog

donkey

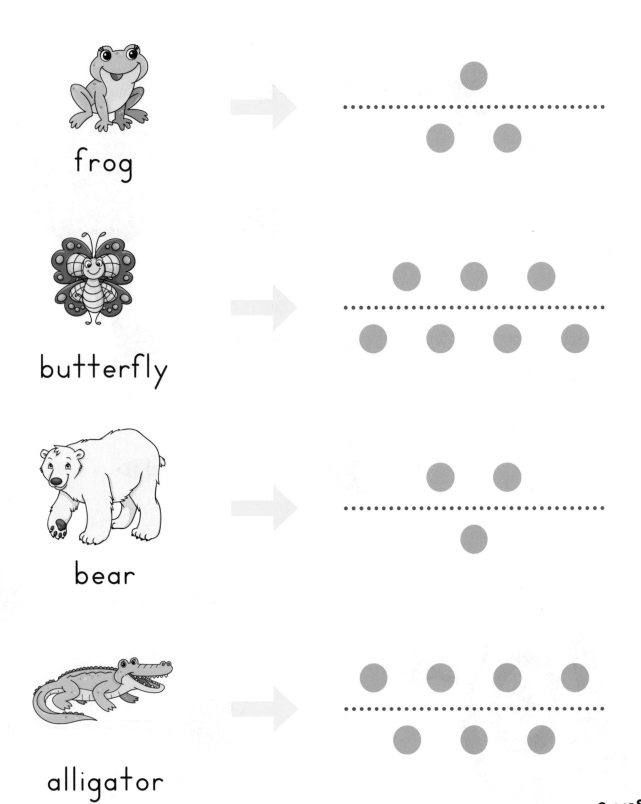

frog

butterfly

bear

alligator

Left or Right

For each arrow, **write** either L or R to show which direction it is pointing.

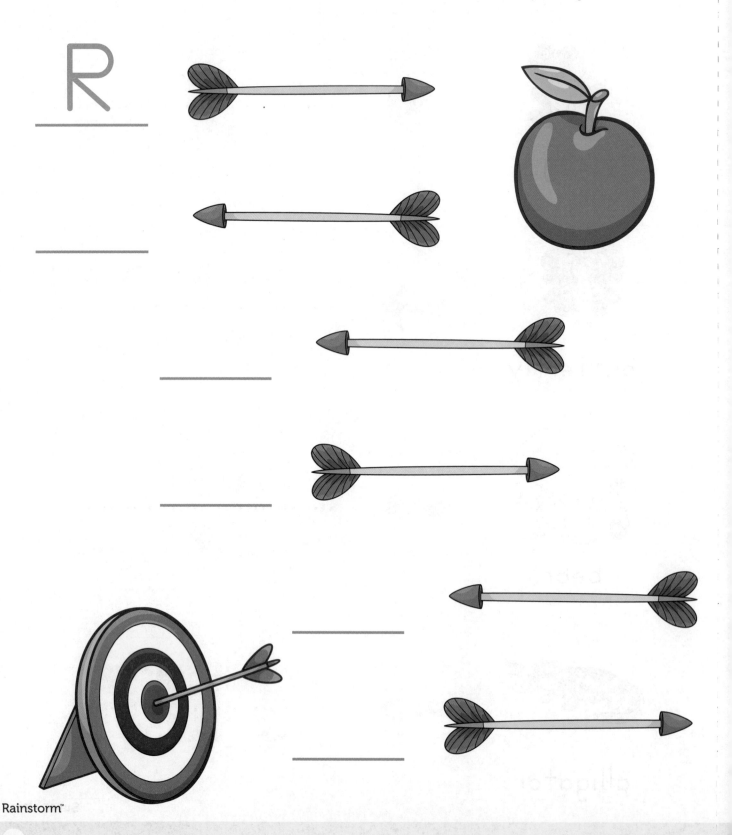

R

_____

_____

_____

_____

_____

_____

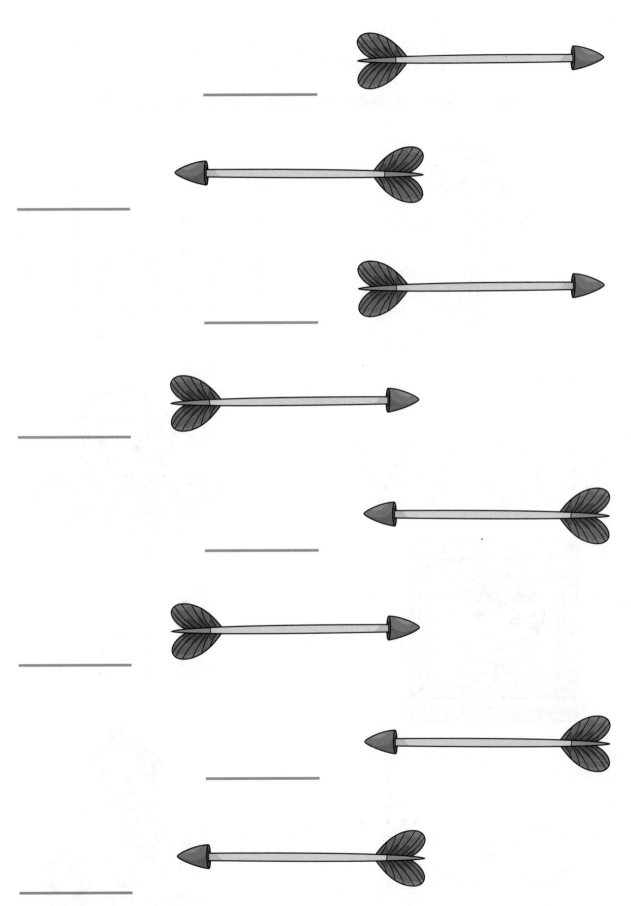

Position Words

Trace the placement words below and **say** them out loud as you trace.

high

low

in

out

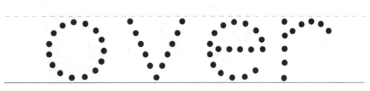

over

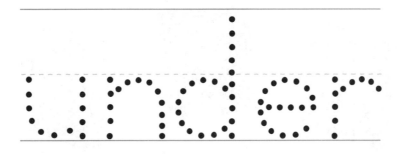

under

So Many Books!

Trace the lines to find which book each child is reading.

CAKES

STORY TIME

FLOWERS

DINOSAURS

SPORTS

Opposites

Trace the word under each picture.

over

high

inside

under

low

outside

old

young

Rocket Shapes

Color the shapes on the rocket to match the ones below.

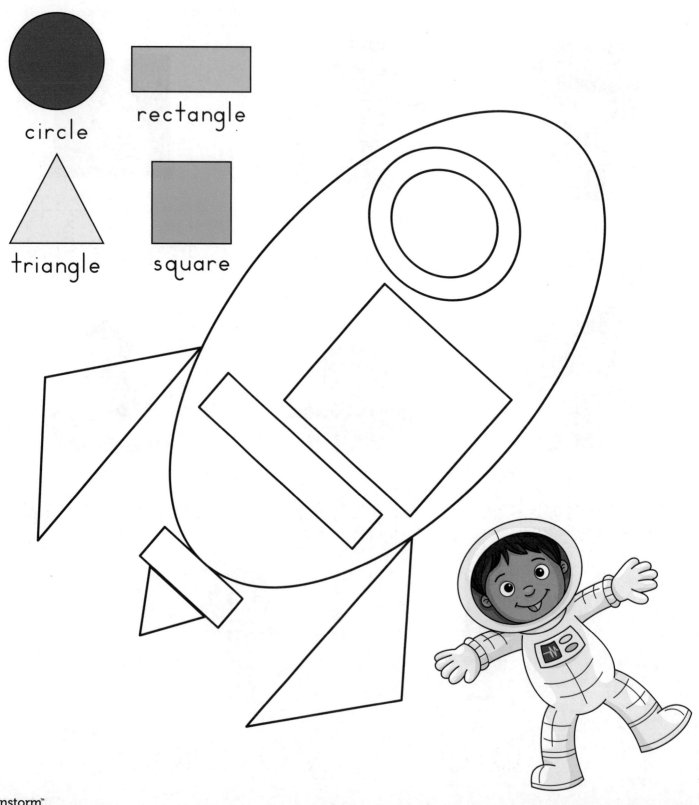

circle

rectangle

triangle

square

Sky Search

Circle the things that are found in the sky.
Draw an X over the things that are not found in the sky.

Melting Match

Draw a line to match each ice cream with its melted puddle.

Hot and Cold

Use red to **circle** the things that are hot. Use blue to **circle** the things that are cold.

Hot   Cold

Weather Words

Trace the weather words below.

snow

wind

rain

sun

Winter or Summer?

Circle the summer clothes with yellow.
Circle the winter clothes with blue.

Summer   Winter

Packing for Space

Pretend you are an astronaut preparing for takeoff into space.
Circle the items you should pack on both pages.

Heavy or Light?

In each pair, **circle** the object that is heavier than the other.

pillow   couch

cow   rabbit

feather   rock

Float or Sink?

Some things float in water and some things sink.
Color the objects that will float.

Dino Bones

Circle the dinosaur that matches the skeleton.

Electric Gadgets

Circle the objects that need electricity to work.

Slow to Fast

Place these pictures in order from fastest to slowest.
Write the numbers **1**, **2**, and **3** to order the pictures.

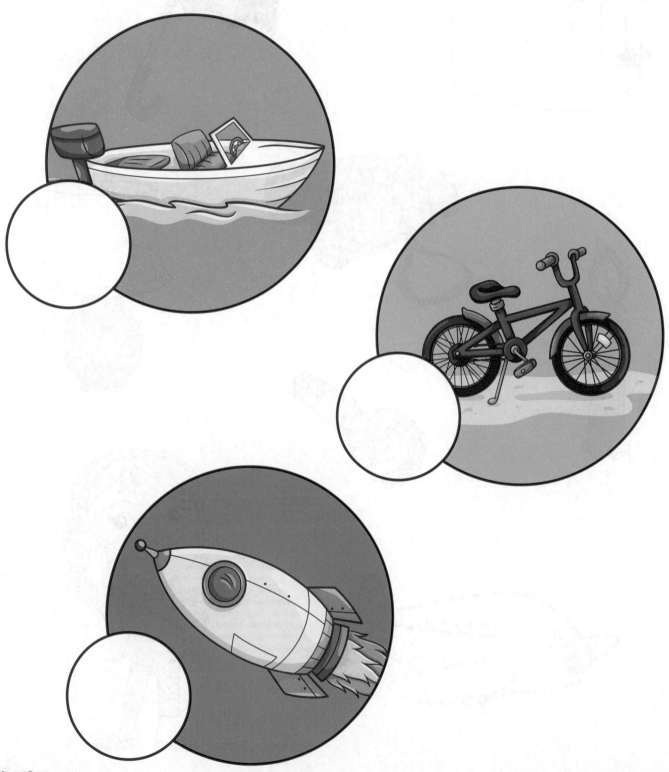

Flying High

Circle the objects that can fly.

Path to the Moon

Help the rocket reach the moon by solving the maze.

Smells Good

Some things have strong smells. **Circle** the things that smell good to you.

Digging Fun

Draw an X on the deepest hole.

Footprint Detective

Draw a line between the shoe and its matching print.

Rainbow Dots

Sunshine and rain combine to create rainbows.
Finish coloring the rainbow by connecting each row of dots with its matching color.

Liquid or Solid Foods

Some foods are liquids that you drink and others are solids that you eat.
Cross out the solid foods below.

Above, On, Below

Some objects are above the water, some on it, and some below.
Point to each object and say where they are. Then **color** them!

Planet Match

Draw a line to connect each planet with its other half.

Venus

Earth

Mars

Saturn

Uranus

Neptune

Something's Different: Fossils

There are ten differences between these two pictures! **Find** and **circle** them.

What Color is it?

Trace the name of the color that describes each picture pair.

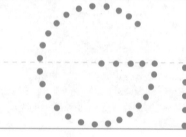

What Color is it?

Trace the name of the color that describes each picture pair.

Get Creative!

Draw a line to match the artwork with the material used to make it.

Color The Crown

Color all the diamonds in the crown.

Grid Art

Use the grid to **finish** the picture.
How many legs should this octopus have?

Where is My Wing?

Draw a line to match each butterfly with its missing wing.

Color with Green

Color these pictures green.

Finish the Picture

Make these helicopters look the same.
Draw the missing parts on the bottom helicopter.

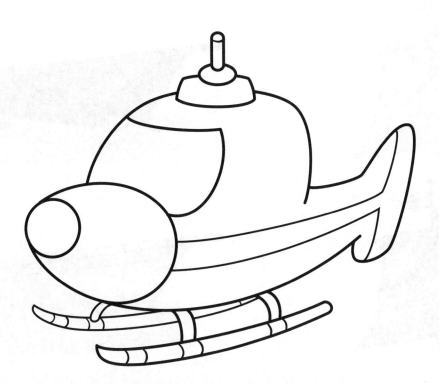

Boats Afloat!

Draw a line between the sails and their matching sailboats.

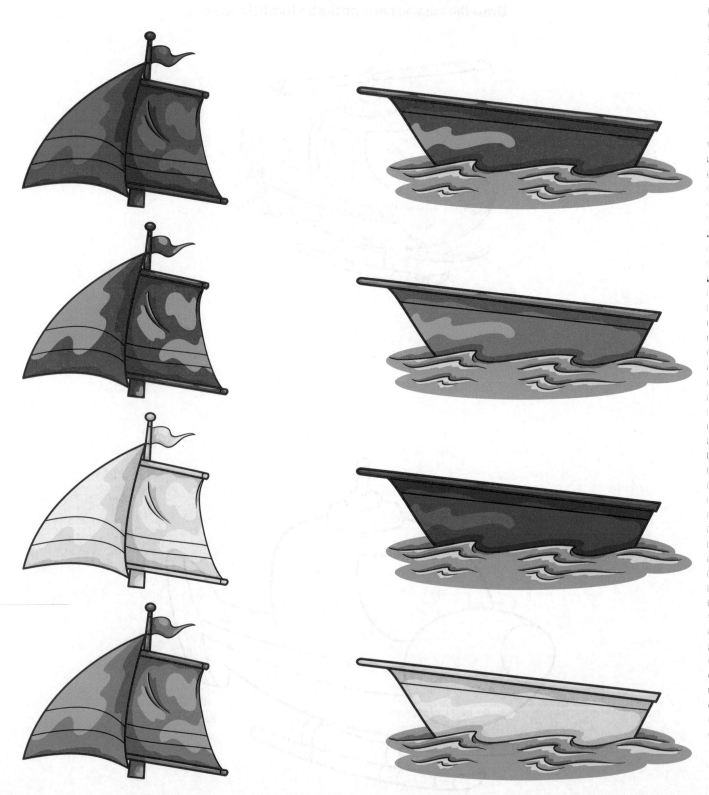

Missing Wings

Draw wings on the dragon's body.

Super Smart

Sketch a Bug

Follow the steps to **draw** your own ladybug.

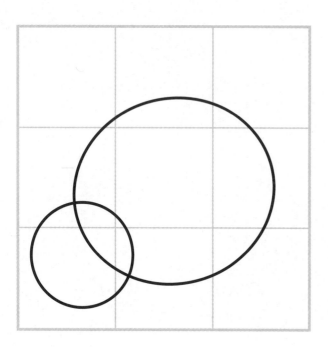

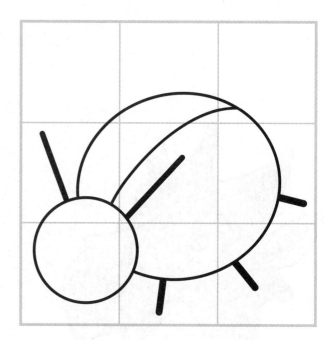

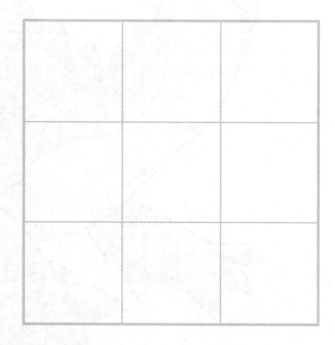

Mixing Colors

Mixing yellow and blue paint makes a new color.
Trace the name of the new color.

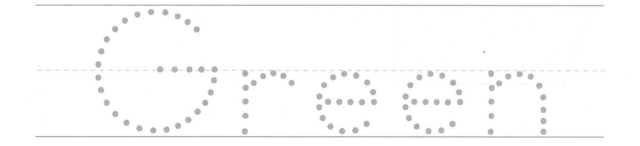

Sketch a Boat

Follow the steps to **draw** your own tugboat.

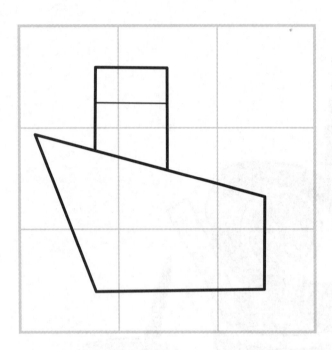

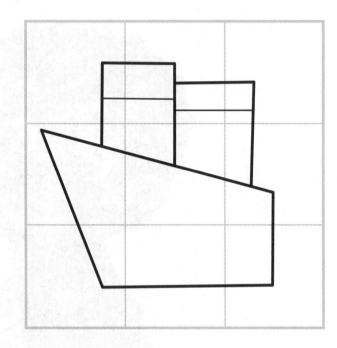

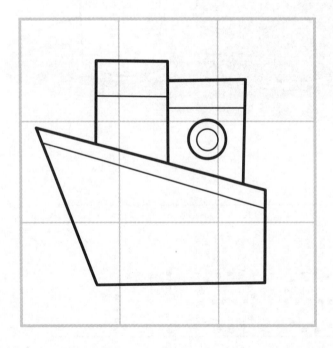

Beading Patterns

Follow the pattern to **color** the beads.

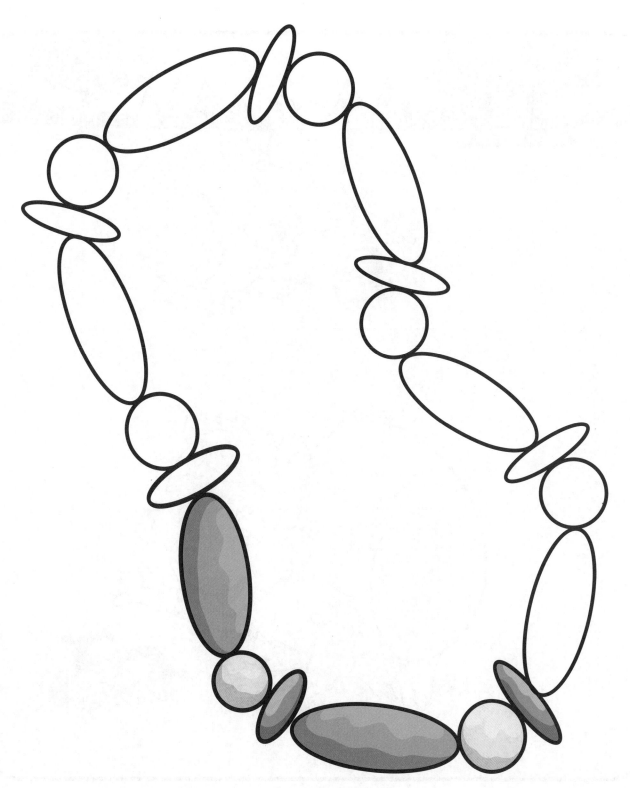

Missing Tails

These squirrels are missing their bushy tails. **Draw** their tails.

Finish the Robots

Use the top picture to help you finish **drawing** the robot.

Sketch a Panda

Use the top picture to help you **finish** the drawings below.

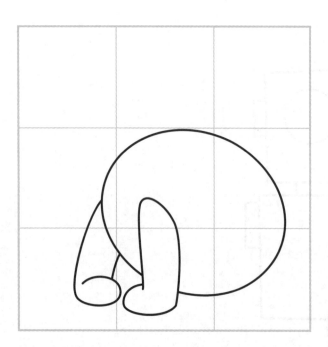

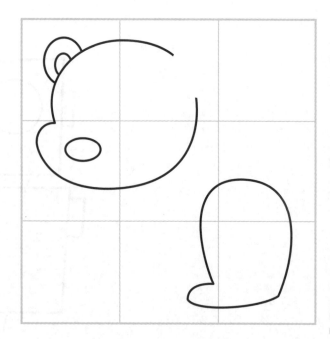

Summer Sprinkler Splash

Use the color words to help you **finish** coloring the picture.

Color Words: Yellow

Color the word using the color yellow.

Color Words: Pink

Color the word using the color pink.

Color Words: Orange

Color the word using the color orange.

Color Words: Purple

Color the word using the color purple.

Color Words: Black

Color the word using the color black.

Color Words: White

Color the word using the color white.

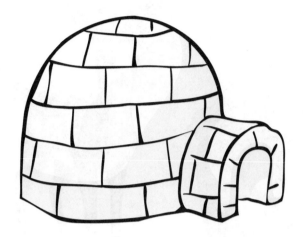

white

Color Words: Brown

Color the word using the color brown.

Color Words: Gray

Color the word using the color gray.

Color Words: Red

Color the word using the color red.

Red

Color Words: Green

Color the word using the color green.

Color Words: Blue

Color the word using the color blue.

Red Chalk

Circle the pictures that are drawn with red chalk.

Monster Splash

Draw a line to connect each monster with its matching color splash.

Colorful Caterpillar

Color the caterpillar by copying the color dot in each section.

Cupcake Decorating

Decorate these cupcakes by drawing colorful sprinkles, fruit, and candy on them.

Draw A Cat

Follow the steps using the grid to draw a cat. Then **color** it.

Step 1
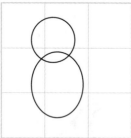

Step 2
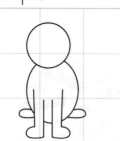

Step 3

Step 4

Draw A Dog

Follow the steps using the grid to draw a dog. Then **color** it.

Step 1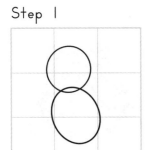

Step 2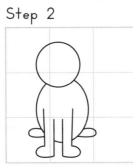

Step 3

Step 4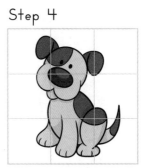

Draw A Frog

Follow the steps using the grid to draw a frog. Then **color** it.

Step 1

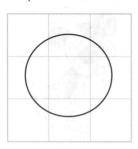

Step 2

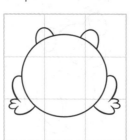

Step 3

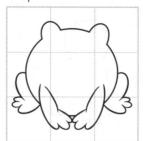

Step 4

Draw A Bird

Follow the steps using the grid to draw a bird. Then **color** it.

Step 1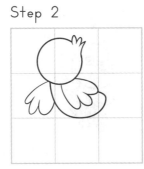

Step 2

Step 3

Step 4

Buzzing Bees

Follow the tracing lines to connect the bees with the flowers.

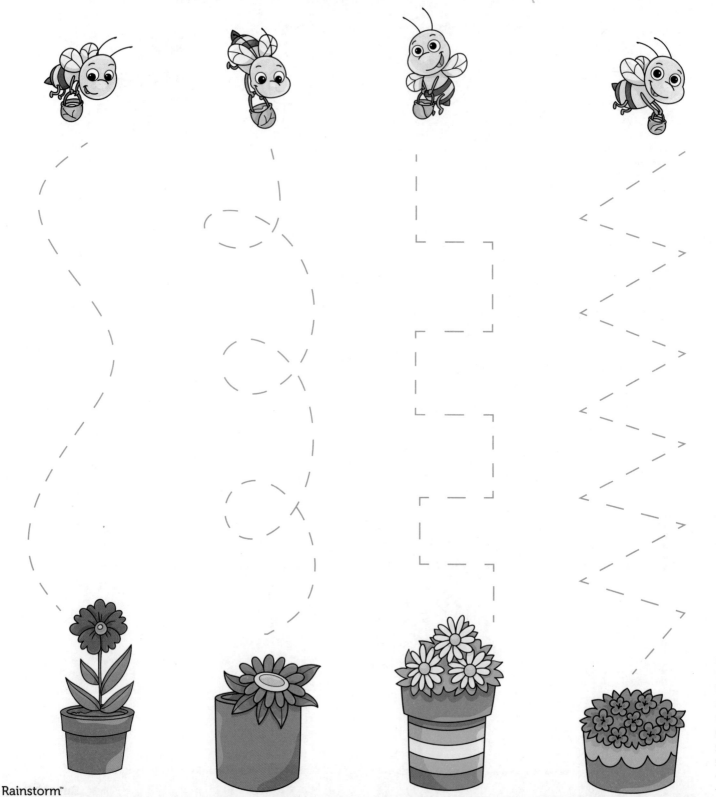

Mix the Colors

Use the key below to **color** in each circle.

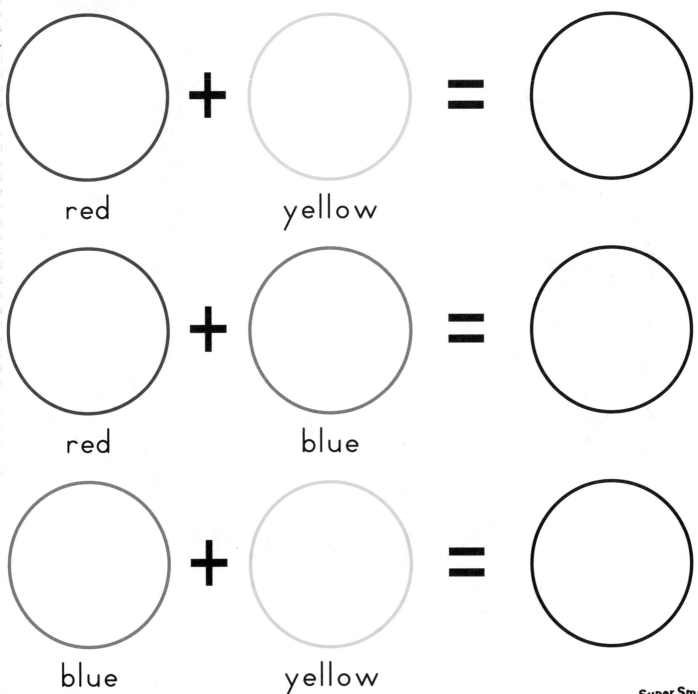

red + yellow =

red + blue =

blue + yellow =

Monster Faces

Draw a face on this monster. Then **color** it!

Fish Paths

Draw lines to help these fish get to the worms.

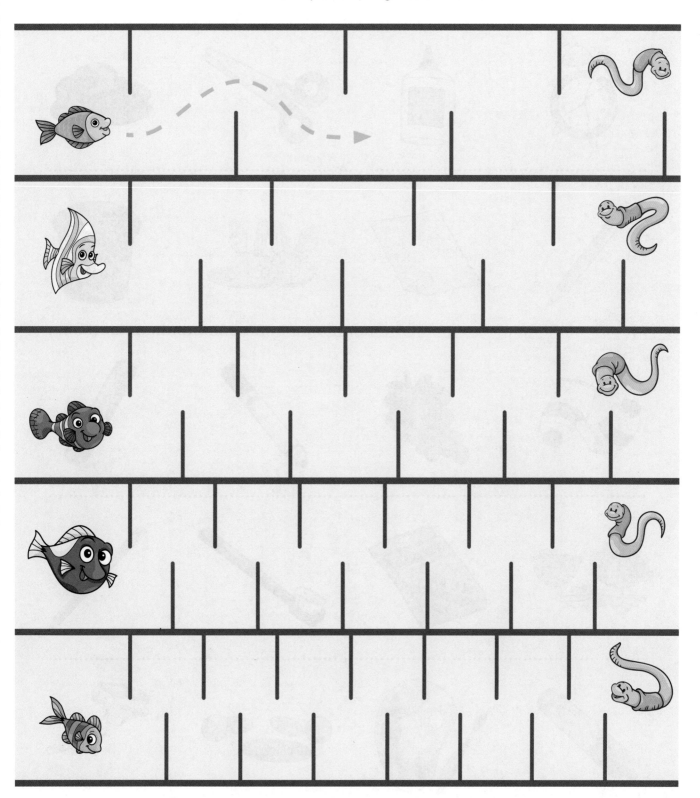

Odd One Out

Find the object in each row that isn't an art tool and **cross it out**.

  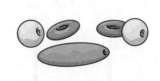 

Odd Fairy Out

For each row, **cross out** the fairy that doesn't match the others.

How Are You Feeling?

Draw a face to show how you feel today.
Draw a second face to show how a friend or parent feels.

Rainstorm™

Happy   Mad   Sad   Shy

Home Sweet Home

Where does each item belong in the house?
Draw a line between each item and the and the room it belongs in..

Day and Night

What do you do during the day and what do you do at night?
Draw a line to connect each activity with the sun or moon.

Toss It!

Where should you put your garbage?
Check the box for the pictures that show good behavior.

Sharing

Check the box for the picture that shows good manners.

Young and Old

Place these pictures in order, from youngest bear to oldest bear.
Write the numbers **1**, **2**, and **3** to put these pictures in order from youngest to oldest.

Theater Silliness

Circle all the silly things that don't belong on the stage.

Bake a Cake!

Write the numbers **1**, **2**, **3**, and **4** to put the pictures in the correct order to bake a cake.

Cleaning Time

Draw a line to connect each item to where it should be put away.

Birthday Treats

Circle the foods that you would share with a friend at a birthday party.

Sharing with Friends

A friend forgot his lunch.
Check the box next to the picture that shows how to help.

Crossing the Street

Read the rules. Circle the sign that means it is okay to cross the street.

RULES:
1. Look both ways twice
2. Wait for walk signal
3. Walk quickly
4. Hold a friend's hand

What to Wear?

Circle the clothes you would wear if you were going to swim lessons.

Taking Care

Circle the things that you can use to take care of a sick friend.

Toy Time Maze

Help this boy find his toy box by **completing** the maze.

START

FINISH

TOY BOX

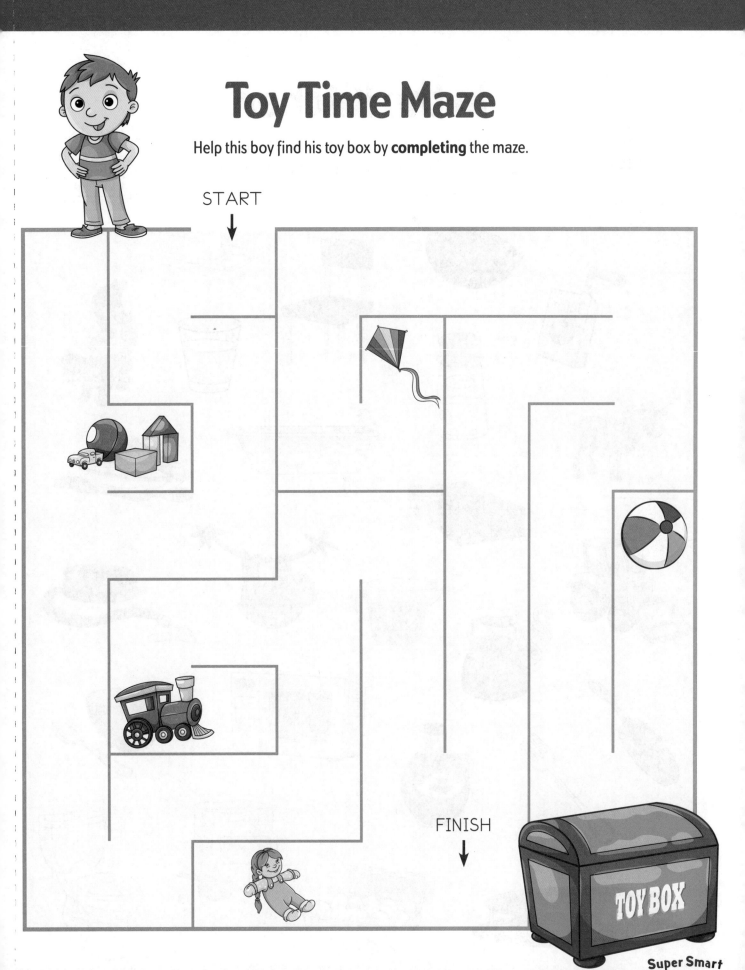

Super Smart

In the Kitchen

Which items below are not found in a kitchen?
Cross out the items below that do not belong in a kitchen.

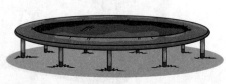

Totem Pole Coloring

Native Americans are well known for totem poles, which are carvings made out of tree logs.
They have important animal designs on them that tell a story.
Color the totem pole below and then **finish** the maze.

Months of the Year

Count how many months there are in a year and **write** the number in the box below.
Then **circle** the month you were born in!

January

February

March

April

May

June

July

August

September

October

November

December

Number of months:

Write a Letter

Pretend you are writing a letter to a friend.
Place these pictures in order by **writing** the numbers **1**, **2**, and **3** in the circles below.

World Food

Trace the lines to see where each food comes from.

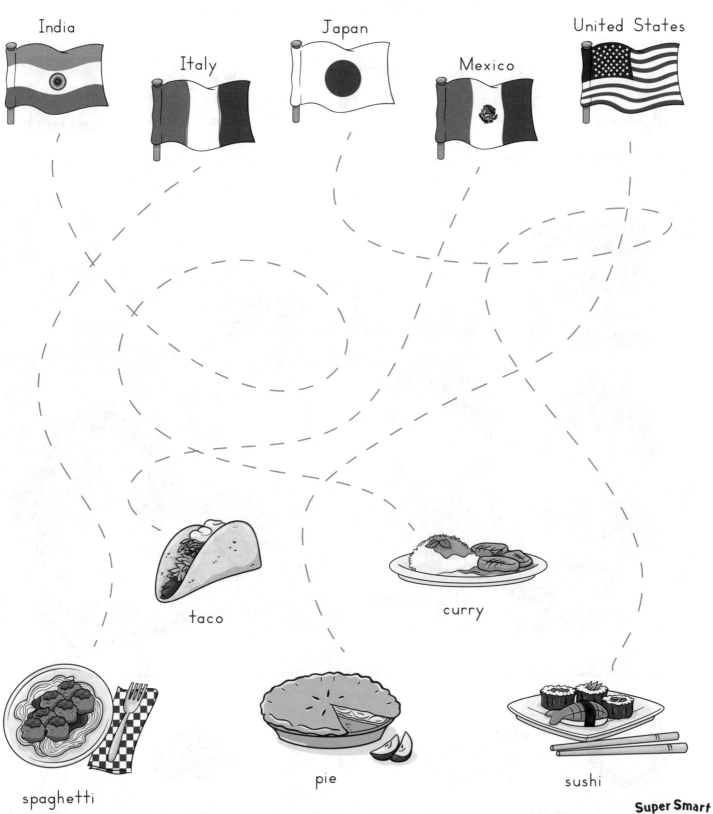

India

Italy

Japan

Mexico

United States

taco

curry

spaghetti

pie

sushi

Time for Preschool

Preschool classrooms are filled with many tools to help you learn.
Can you **find** and **circle** these images in the picture below?

Traffic Light

Color the traffic light below using red for stop, yellow for wait, and green for go.
Then **color** the bus scene below.

stop

wait

go

1

Learn how to write your numbers
by **tracing** the outlines on the following pages.

one cow

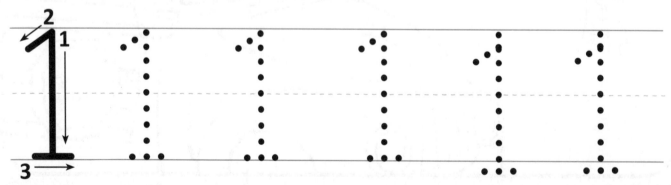

2 two horses

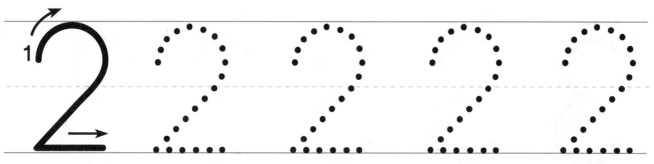

3 three pigs

3 3 3 3 3

4 four chickens

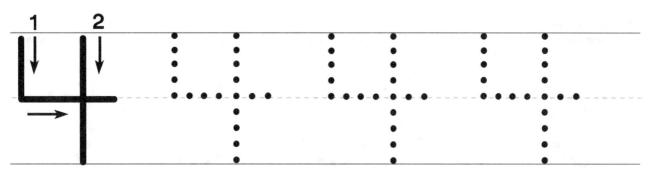

5 five goats

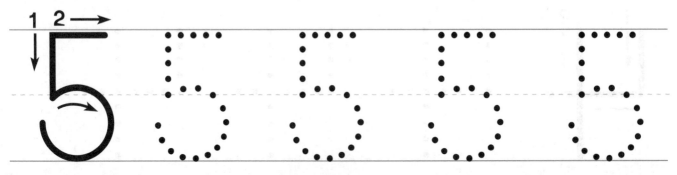

5 5 5 5 5

6 six sheep

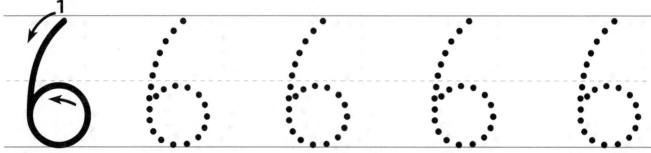

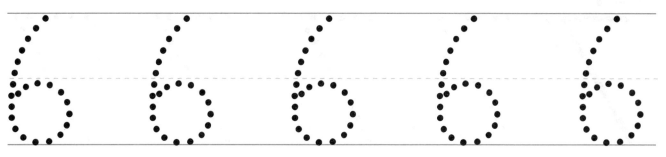

7 seven cats

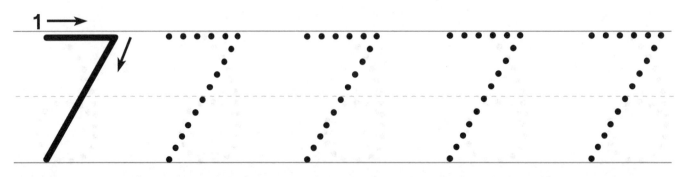

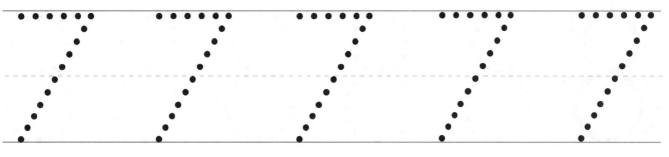

8 eight dogs

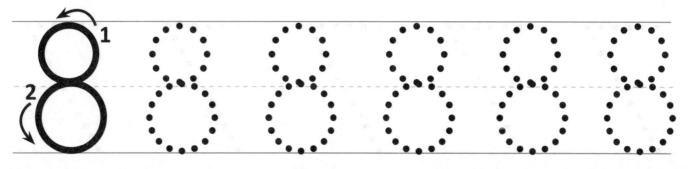

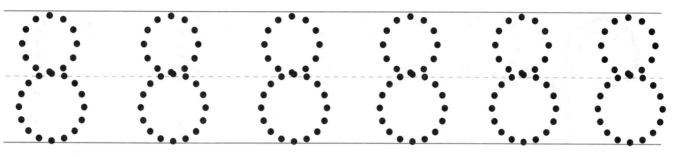

9 nine ducks

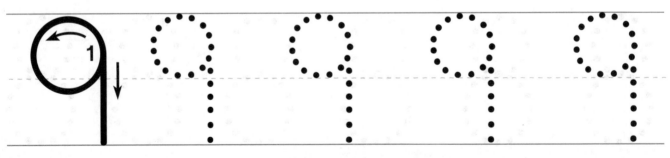

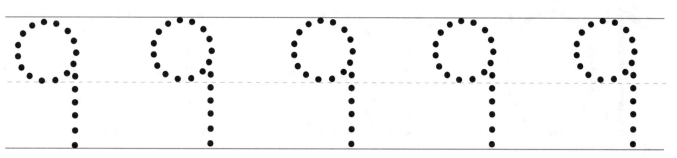

10 ten frogs

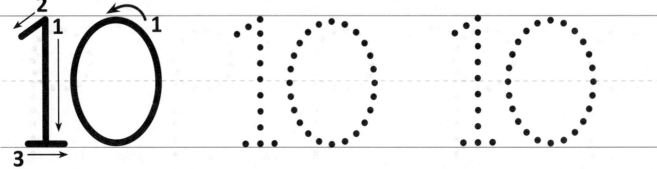

10 10 10

Numbers and Words

Trace each number and number word for 1-10.

1 one

2 two

3 three

4 four

5 five

6 six

7 seven

8 eight

9 nine

10 ten

Counting Fabulous Fruit

Circle the correct number of fruit to go with the shopping list.
Then **write** the number next to the picture

	Shopping List
	• 5 Apples • 8 Oranges • 2 Pears

_____

- - - - - - - - - - - -

_____

_____

- - - - - - - - - - - -

_____

_____

- - - - - - - - - - - -

_____

Counting Tasty Treats

Circle the correct number of party treats to go with the shopping list.
Then **write** the number next to the picture.

	Shopping List
	•3 Cakes •7 Cupcakes •4 Candies

_____

- - - - - - - - - - - -

_____

_____

- - - - - - - - - - - -

_____

_____

- - - - - - - - - - - -

_____

Royal Counting

How many royal jewels below are BIG
and how many are small?
Count how many for each color group.

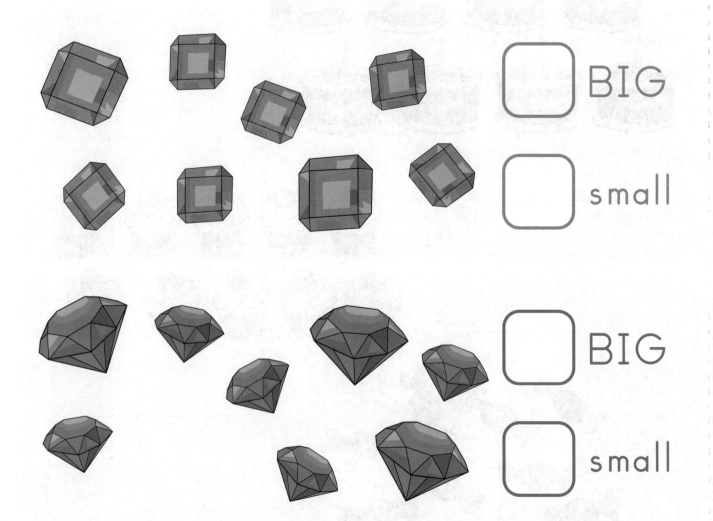

BIG

small

BIG

small

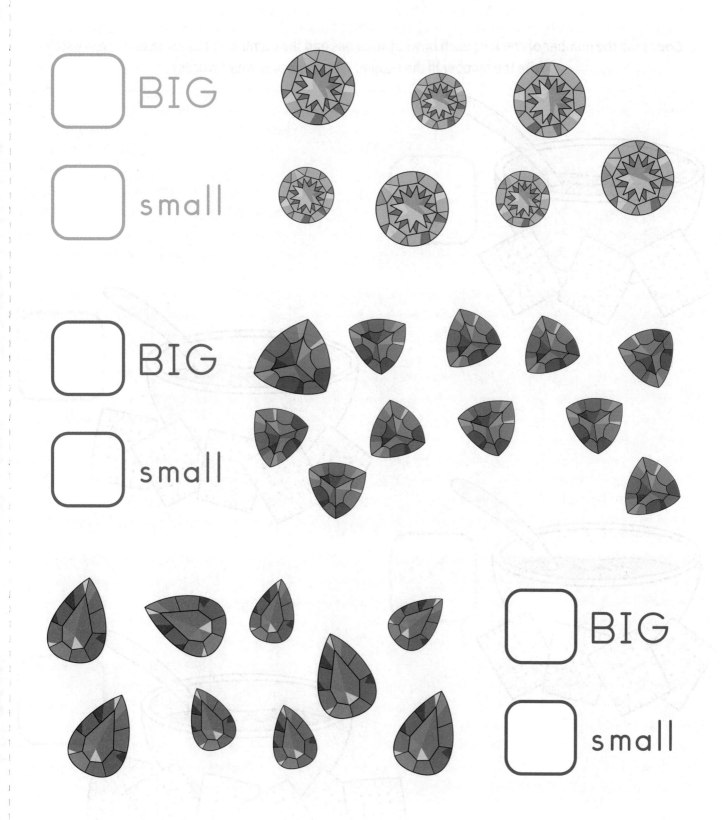

BIG

small

BIG

small

BIG

small

Counting Snacks

Count the the number of crackers each bowl of soup has and the number of raisins on each celery stalk. **Write** the number in the square. Which snack is your favorite?

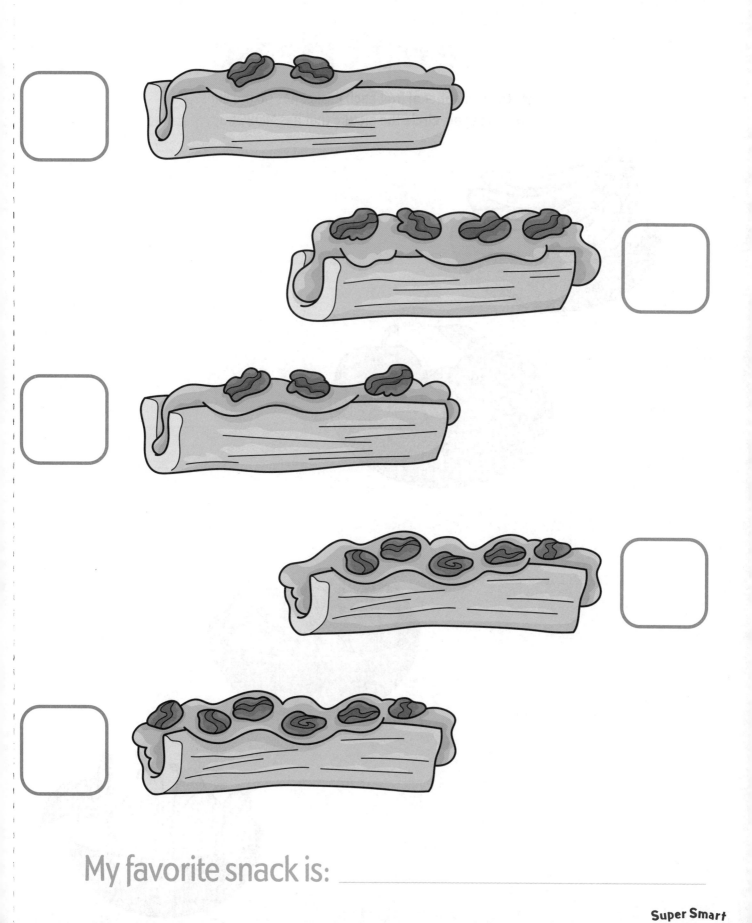

My favorite snack is: _____

More Fruit Please!

Write the number of fruit each basket has on the lines.
For each pair, **circle** the picture that has MORE fruit.

Counting Candy!

Write the number of candies each container has on the lines.
For each pair, **circle** the picture that has FEWER candies.

_____

_____

_____

_____

Match the Part to the Whole

Draw a line between each item and its missing part.

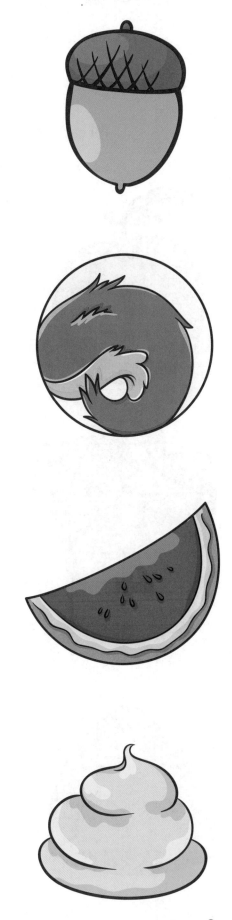

Garden Fun

Practice number order!
For each row of pictures, **write** the missing numbers in the empty spaces.

Space Numbers

Practice number order!
For each row of pictures, **write** the missing numbers in the empty spaces.

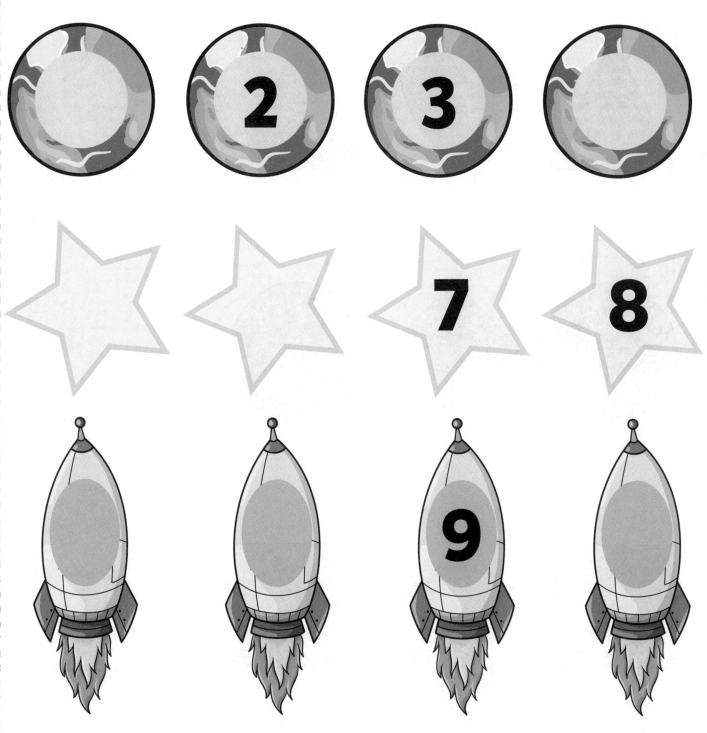

Pattern Perfect

What is the pattern? Figure out which shape should come next in each row of pictures.
Then **draw** a picture of it.

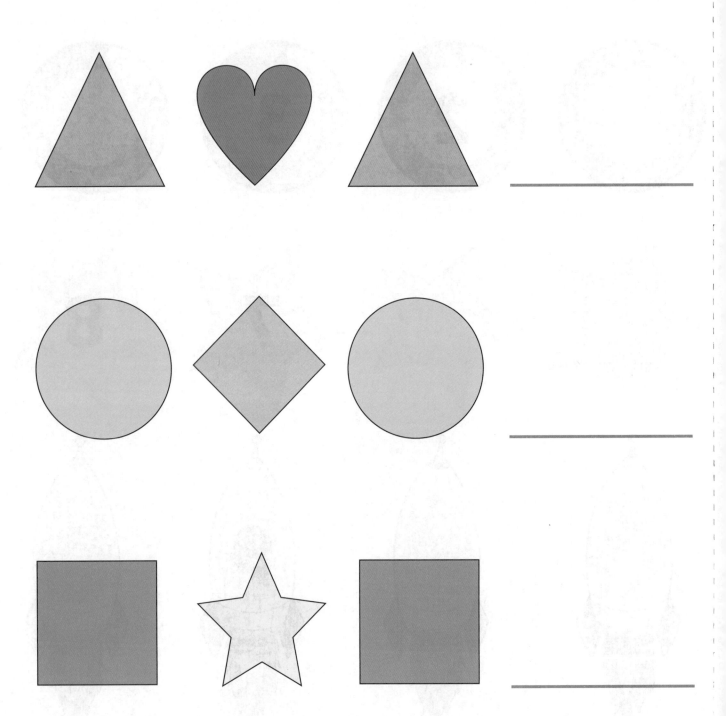

Shapes on a Farm

Draw a line from each shape outline to the similar shapes in the farm picture.

Super Shapes

Trace each shape.
Then **color** each shape to look like the matching object.

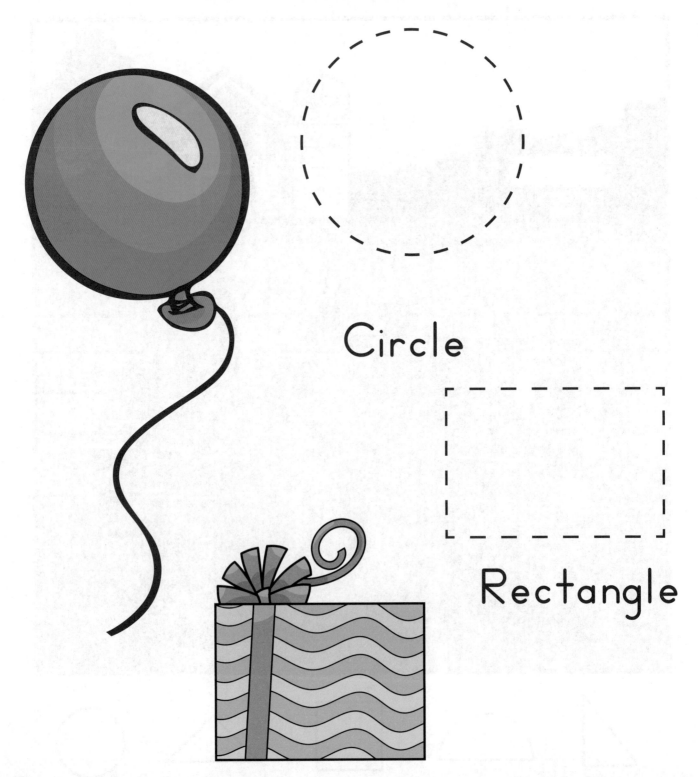

Circle

Rectangle

Square

Triangle

Colorful Shapes

Color each shape inside the big box.
Use the key below to help you **color** the shapes in the big box.

 Squares – Red

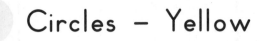 Circles – Yellow

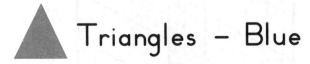 Triangles – Blue

 Rectangles – Orange

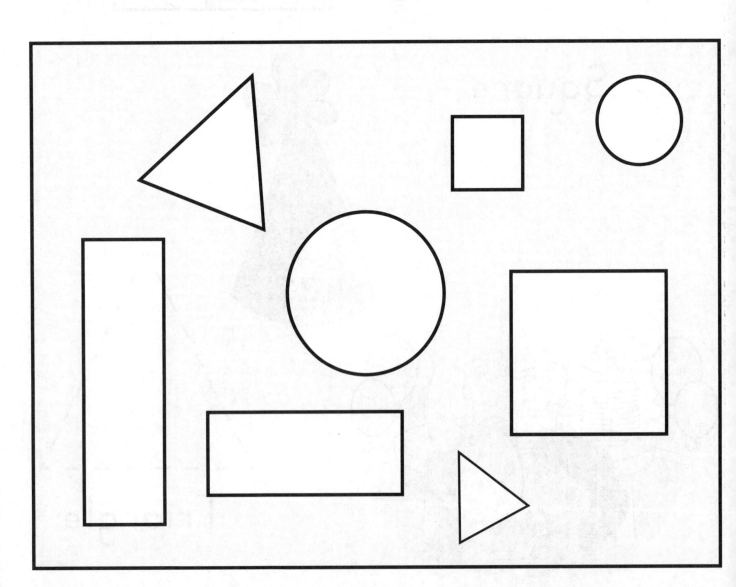

Treasure Hunt

Find the treasure by following the path that has this pattern:

☆ → ■ → ▲ → ●

Similar Shapes

Draw a line between objects with similar shapes.

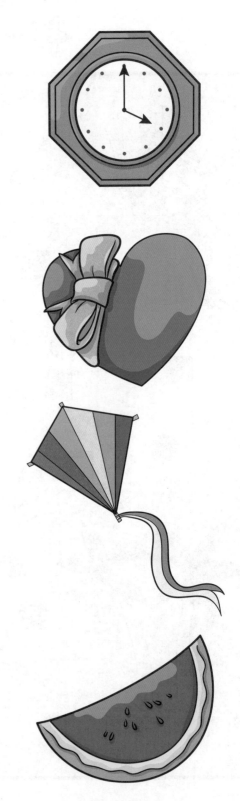

Squares Galore

Trace the squares. Then **color** them to match the pictures.

Tracing Shapes: Circles

Trace the circle shapes. **Color** them to make more lemon and lime slices.

Tracing Shapes: Squares

Trace the square shapes. **Color** them to make more waffles.

Tracing Shapes: Triangles

Trace the triangle shapes. **Color** them to make more dinosaur spikes.

Tracing Shapes: Hearts

Trace the heart shapes. **Color** them to make more cookies.

Tracing Shapes: Stars

Trace the star shapes. **Color** them to make more stars.

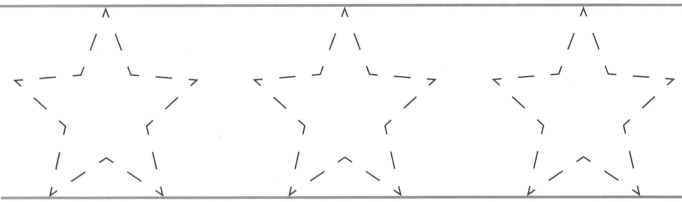

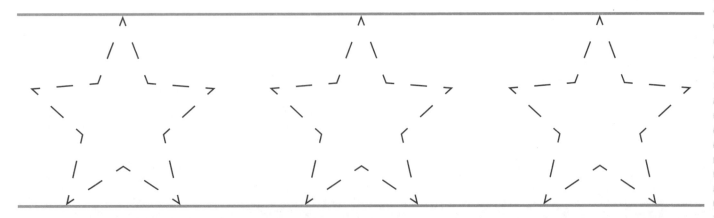

Tracing Shapes: Ovals

Trace the oval shapes. **Color** them to make more watermelons.

How Many Teeth?

Count how many teeth each alligator has. Circle the alligator with the most teeth.

She Sells Seashells

Count the number of each type of shell. Write the number in the boxes below..

Bug Count

Count how many of each type of insect you see on the next page.
Write the numbers in the boxes below.

Counting Fingers

Match each kid with the number of fingers they are holding up.

6 7 8 9 10

Counting Marbles

Fill in the bag of marbles by using the key below.

2 Red   3 Blue   4 Yellow
1 Green   1 Purple   2 Orange

Catch a Fish

How many different fish did this boy catch?
Count how many of each color and **write** the number in the boxes below.

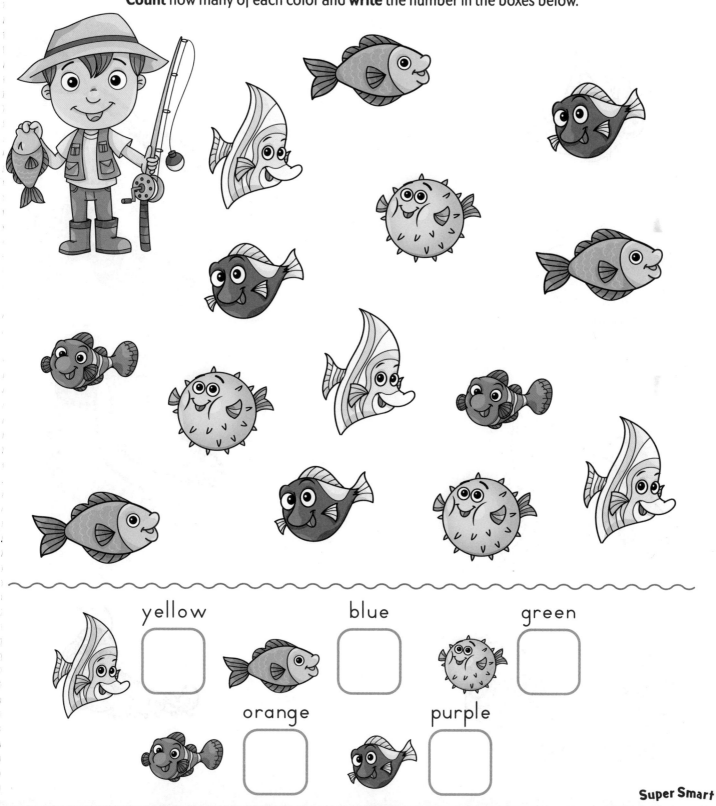

yellow

blue

green

orange

purple

Marvelous Matching

Draw a line to connect the object that make a pair..

Doghouse Match

Draw a line to connect each doghouse with its missing roof.

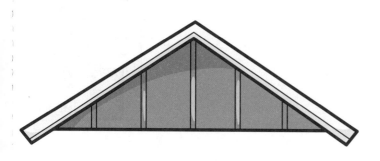

Super Smart

Houses and Hats

These hats and houses have the same patterns.
Draw a line to connect each hat to its matching house.

Rainstorm™

Present Surprise!

Guess what is inside each birthday present. **Draw** a line to connect each present with the toy.

Dino Height

Use the ruler to **measure** each dinosaur. **Write** its height in the square.
Which one is taller?

14 ft

13 ft

12 ft

11 ft

10 ft

9 ft

8 ft

7 ft

6 ft

5 ft

4 ft

3 ft

2 ft

1 ft

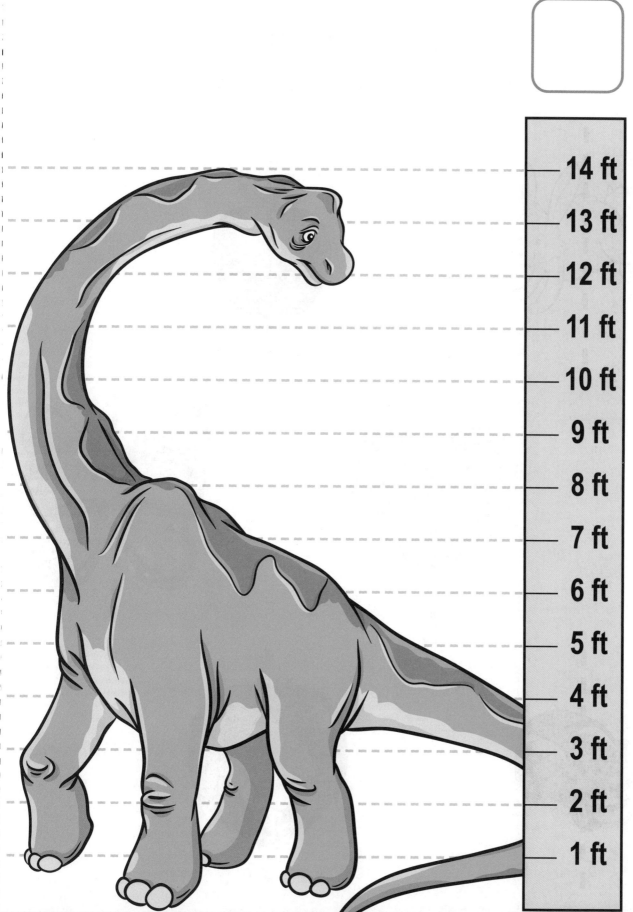

14 ft

13 ft

12 ft

11 ft

10 ft

9 ft

8 ft

7 ft

6 ft

5 ft

4 ft

3 ft

2 ft

1 ft

Super Smart

Mirror Image

Circle the pictures that look the same on both sides of the dotted line.

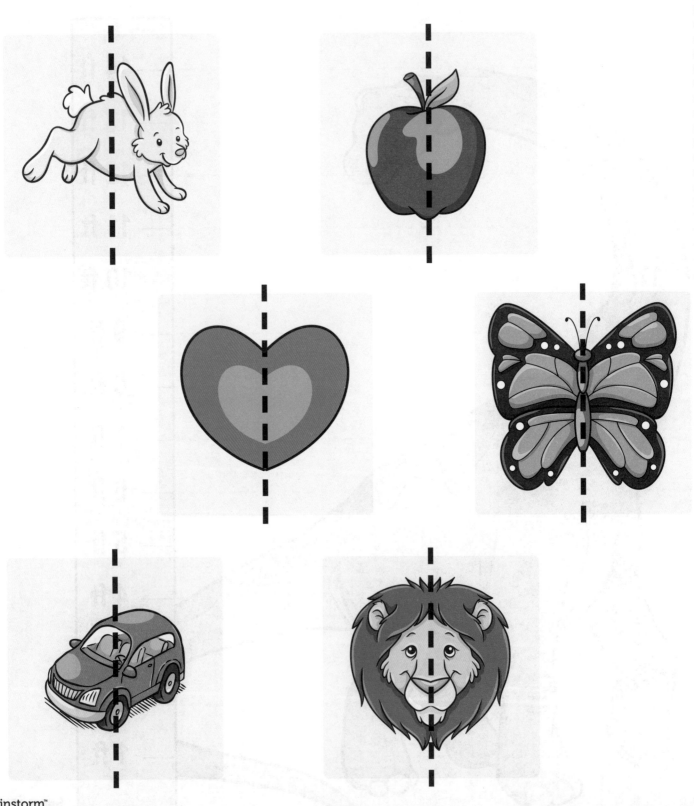

Big and Small Penguins

Circle the biggest penguin and the smallest penguin.

Missing Stripes

This bee is missing her stripes! **Draw** five stripes on her back.

Pack the Backpack

Circle the objects that could fit in the backpack.

Jelly Bean Jar

Count the number of jelly beans of each color. **Write** the numbers below.
Cross out the jelly beans as you count.

Balloon Count

Count the balloons and **write** the number in the box.

Fish Tank Counting

Count how many of each fish you see inside the fish tank and **write** the number in the boxes below.

Watermelon Seeds

Add seeds to these watermelons using the number next to each one.

All About Squares

Color, **trace**, and **connect the dots** of the squares below.

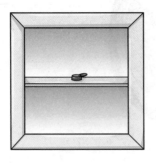

window

sandwich

blanket

checkers board

present

Color

Trace

Connect

Rainstorm™

All About Circles

Color, **trace**, and **connect the dots** of the circles below.

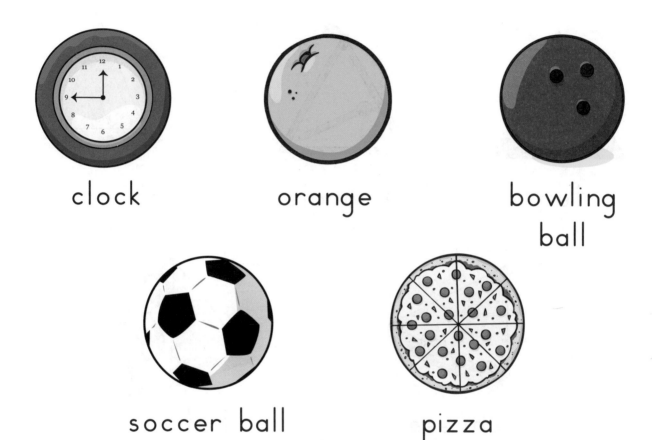

clock

orange

bowling ball

soccer ball

pizza

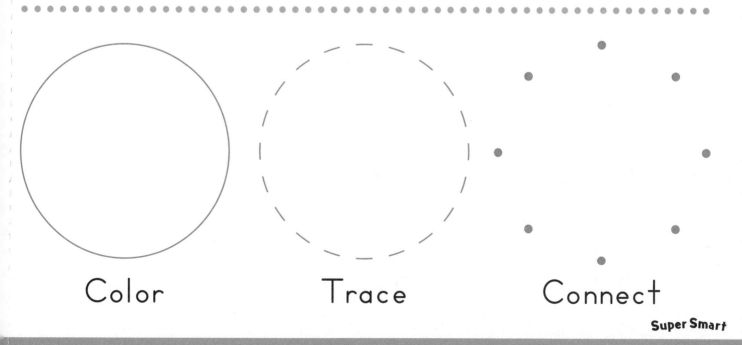

Color

Trace

Connect

All About Triangles

Color, trace, and connect the dots of the triangles below.

tent

triangle

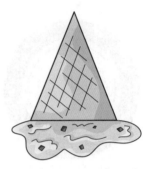

ice cream
cone

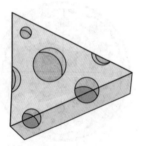

cheese

hat

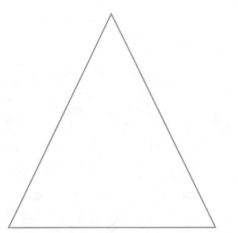

Color

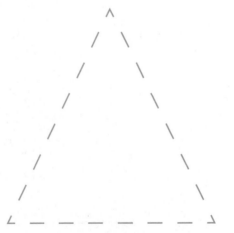

Trace

Connect

All About Ovals

Color, **trace**, and **connect the dots** of the ovals below.

egg

balloon

leaf

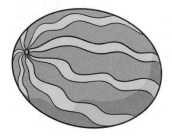

watermelon

rug

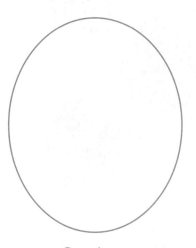

Color

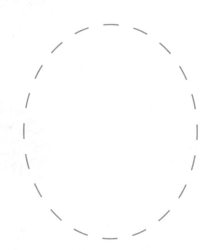

Trace

Connect

Counting Cupcakes

Count how many cupcakes you see in each group and **circle** the correct number below.

2   3   4

7   8   9

5   6   7

3   4   5

Ladybug Match

Draw a line to connect the ladybugs that have the same number of spots.

Super Smart

How Many Scoops?

Count how many scoops each ice cream cone has and **write** the numbers below.

Tallest

Circle the tallest picture in each row.

  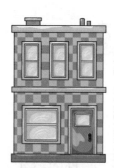 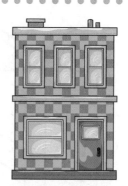

Super Smart

Widest

Circle the widest picture in each row.

How Many Cents?

Trace the number below each coin to find out how many cents each one is worth.

penny

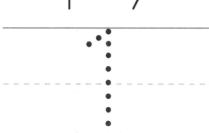

nickel

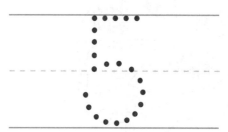

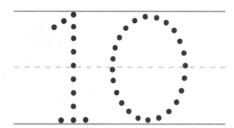

dime

quarter

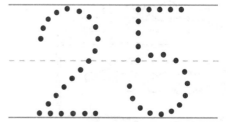

Birthday Cake

Draw a line to connect each cake with its missing slice.

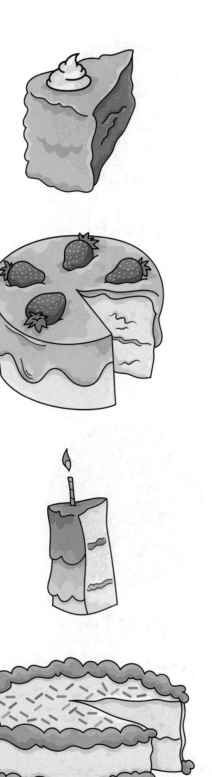

How Many Meatballs?

Count how many meatballs each plate has and **write** the number in the boxes below.

Making Music Together

Trace the name of each rhythm instrument.

Cymbals

Drum

Musical Names

Trace the name of each instrument.

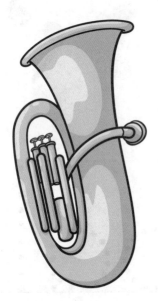

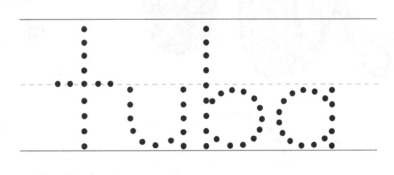

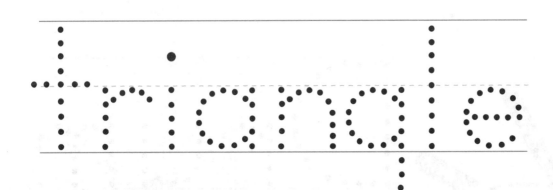

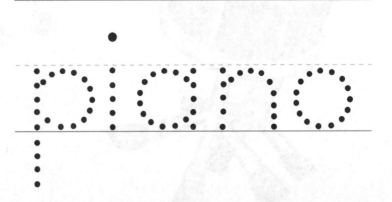

Which One Doesn't Belong?
Strings!

One of these instruments doesn't belong with the others. **Circle** it.

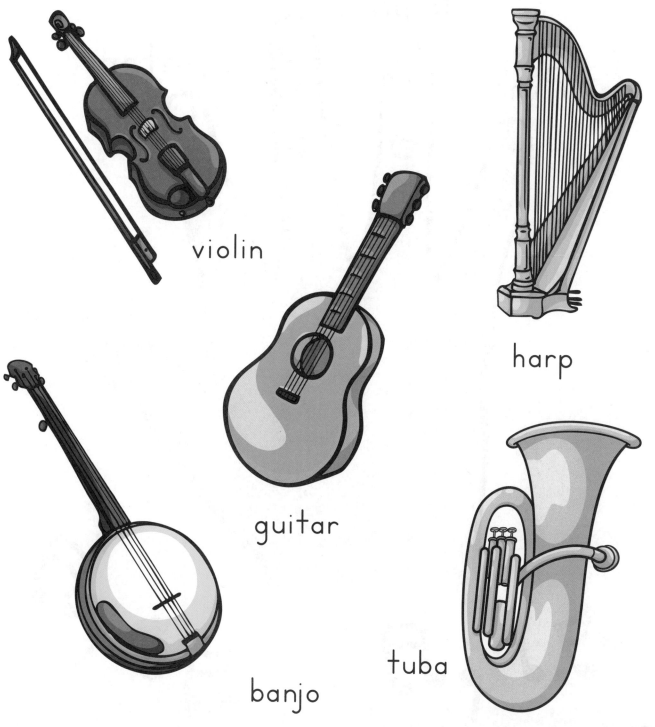

violin

harp

guitar

tuba

banjo

Finger Family

Learn the name of each finger.
Then **wiggle** each of your fingers while you **say** its name.

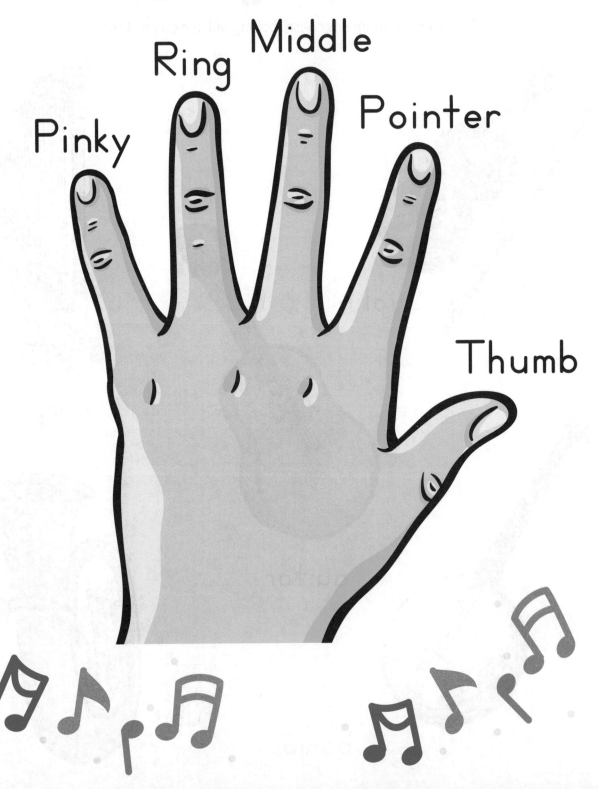

What is Different?

There are 5 differences between the two pictures. **Circle** the things that are different.

Crash! Bang! Boom!

Circle the instruments that makes noise when they are hit.

saxophone

accordian

triangle

drum

cymbals

Find the Beat

Color the shapes the same colors as their dots.

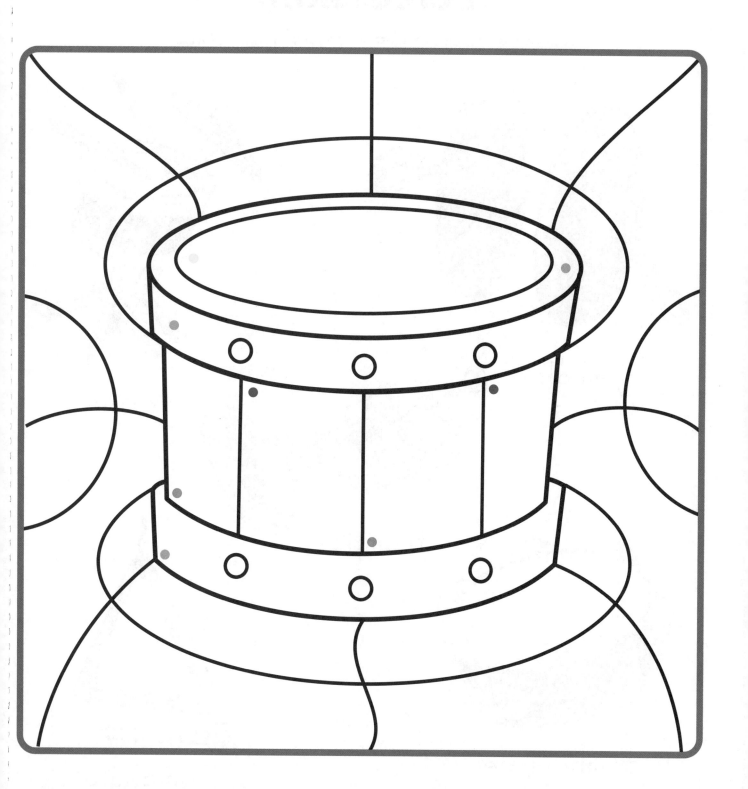

Which One Doesn't Belong? Percussion!

One of these instruments doesn't belong with the others. **Circle** it.

cymbals

drum

trumpet

tambourine

triangle

Rainbow Xylophone

Color each bar a different color.

Hidden Horn

Color the shapes the same colors as their dots.

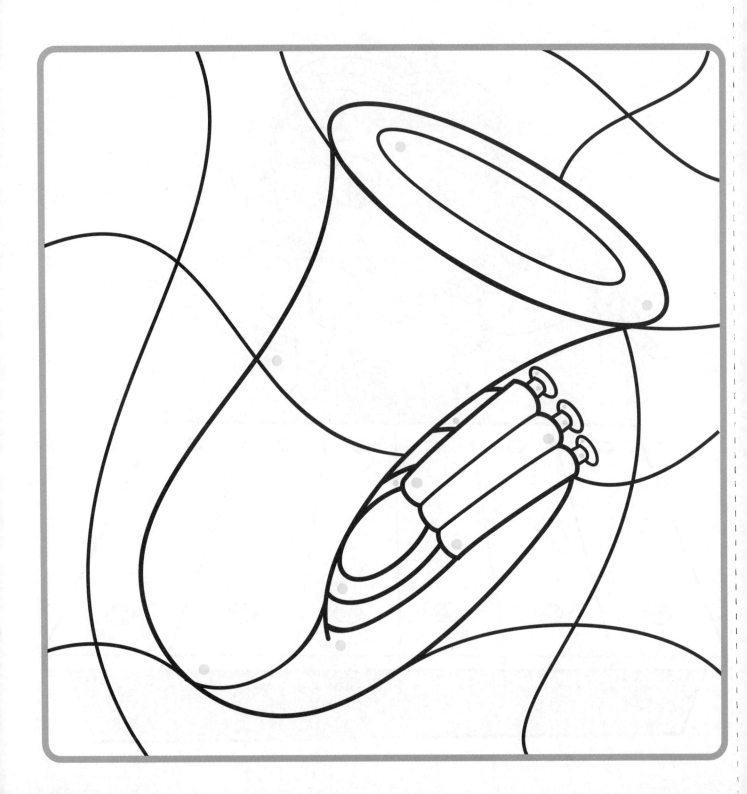

Which One Doesn't Belong? Brass!

One of these instruments doesn't belong with the others. **Circle** it.

trumpet

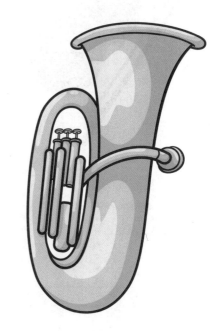

tuba

drum

trombone

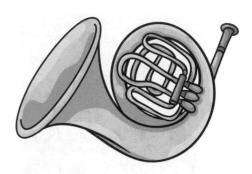

French horn

Shady Music Match

Draw a line between the instruments and their matching shadows.

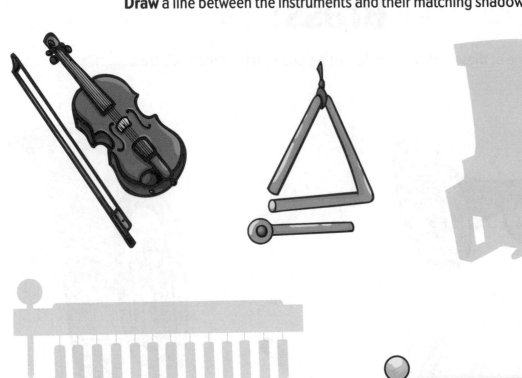

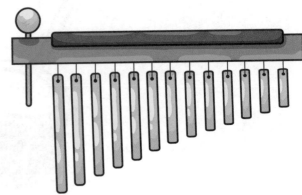

Which One Doesn't Belong?
Woodwinds!

One of these instruments doesn't belong with the others. **Circle** it.

piccolo

flute

saxophone

clarinet

harp

Which are for Blowing?

Circle the instruments that can be played by blowing into them.

harmonica

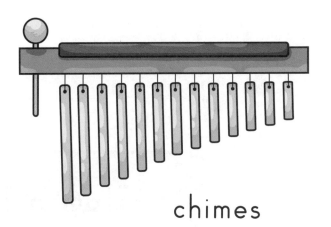

chimes

tambourine

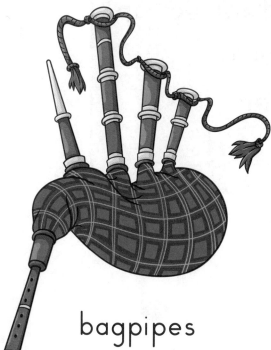

bagpipes

saxophone

I'm a Little Teapot

Sing the song while you **color** the picture on the next page!

I am a little teapot
Short and stout;
Here is my handle,
here is my spout.

When I get all steamed up
Hear me shout;
Tip me over
And pour me out.

Missing Instruments

The instruments below are lost in this messy room! **Circle** each instrument as you find it in the picture.

Animal Sounds

Animals make music too! **Draw** a line to connect the animal with the sound they make. Then practice **saying** it out loud.

ribbit

hoo

roar

woof

meow

moo

neigh

Super Smart

Animals

While exploring a park, lookout for animals.
Circle the animals in the picture below.

Write the number of animals you found.

Shadow Match

Draw a line to connect each leaf with its matching shadow.

Forest Finder

How many forest animals can you find?
Write the number in the box.

Momma and Baby

Draw a line to connect each animal mother with her baby.

Earth Words

Watch out for the hot lava!
Trace the earth — or geology — words on these two pages.

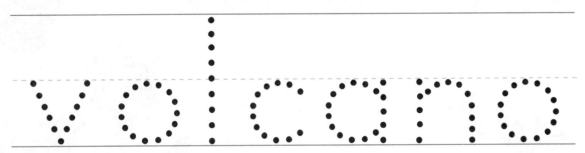

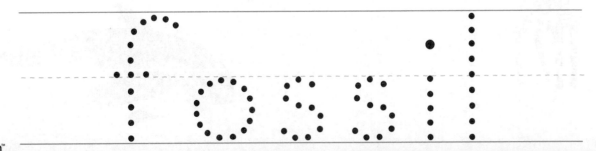

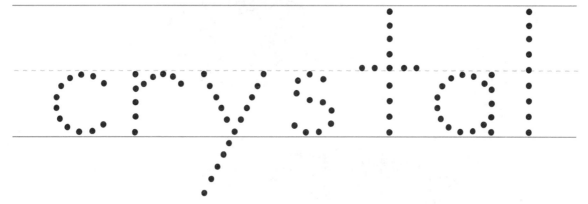

crystal

cave

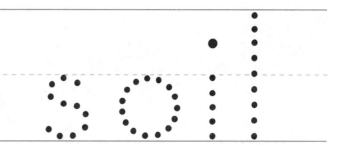

soil

Winged Wonder

What animal did thegirl find? Put a **check** next to the correct animal.

Birds of a Feather

Count the tail feathers on each peacock. Write the number in the boxs below.
Circle the peacock that has the most tail feathers.

Growing Pumpkins

Put these steps in the right order for growing pumpkins.
Write the numbers **1**, **2**, and **3** to put the pictures in the right order for growing pumpkins.

Giraffe Twister

Follow the giraffes' necks to see which one gets to eat the leaves.

Animal House

Trace the dotted lines to help the animals find their way home.

Lounging Lizards

How many lizards can you find hiding in the desert?
Write the number of lizards in the box.

Milk and Honey

Milk and honey both are made by animals.
Draw a line to connect the milk and honey to where they come from.

Firefly Catch

Count the number of fireflies in the jar. Write the number in the box.

Hungry Animals!

Draw a line to connect each hungry animal and its food.

Find the Jaguar!

Find the jaguar hidden with the leopards!

Animal Riddle

Circle the animal that is the answer to the riddle.

I move very slowly.
I sometimes hide in my shell
and I lay my eggs in the sand.
Who am I?

Rainstorm™

Pond Puzzler

How many pond animals can you find?
Write the number in the box.

Animal Tracks

Draw a line between each track and the animal that made it.

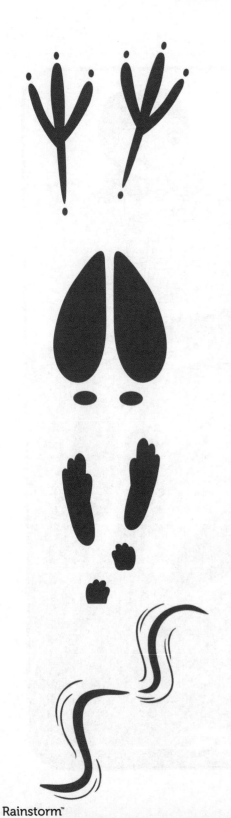

Habitat Trace

Habitats are the different places where animals and plants live.
Trace the word for each habitat.

ocean

forest

pond

desert

Animal Paths

Trace each animal's path.

Wild Pet

Circle the animals you might have as a pet.

Wild Patterns

Finish each animal's pattern!
Find the matching pattern and **draw** it in the circle on each animal.

Nature Walk

Go on a nature walk. What do you see, smell, hear, feel, and taste?
Draw pictures of the things you experienced with your senses.

see	
smell	
hear	
feel	
taste	

Leaf Patterns

Finish the leaf patterns by coloring the leaf that comes next in each row.

Living Things

All living creatures need air, water, and food to survive. **Circle** the living animals below.

Puppies Galore

Draw a line to match the puppy to its mother.

Favorite Veggies

There are so many delicious vegetables out there. Which ones are your favorites?
Draw a check mark to show whether you like, don't like, or have never tried each of the veggies below.

	LIKE!	Don't Like	Never Tried
peas			
beet			
red pepper			
celery			
carrot			
eggplant			
broccoli			
radish			
lettuce			

Animal Names

Write the letter that begins the animal name below.

 = ___ eaver

 = ___ og

 = ___ lephant

 = ___ at

 = __ oat

 = __ nt

 = __ ox

= __ orse

Four Seasons

Trace the seasons' names under each picture. Then **circle** your favorite season.

spring

summer

fall

winter

Circle the Swimmers

Some animals can fly and others can swim. **Circle** the animals below that can swim.

Search and Find Food

The foods below are hidden in the camping picture. **Find** and **circle** them.

Eat a Rainbow

It is healthy to eat foods from all the colors of the rainbow.
Color each rainbow stripe to match the color of the fruit.

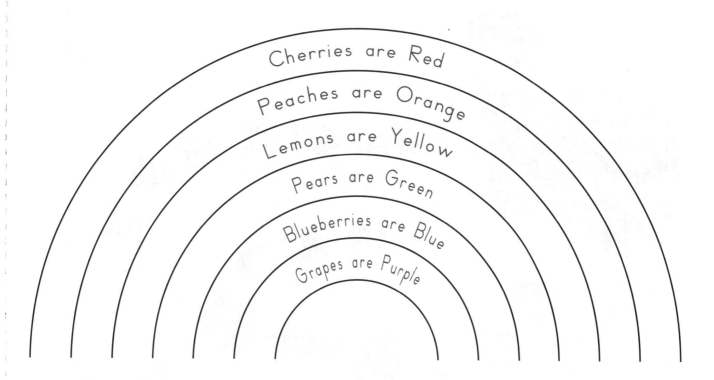

Cherries are Red
Peaches are Orange
Lemons are Yellow
Pears are Green
Blueberries are Blue
Grapes are Purple

Grocery Maze

Solve the maze and help the boy reach the grocery cart by choosing only healthy fruit and vegetables.

Fruit Pits

Fruit may have seeds or a pit inside. **Circle** the fruits that have pits.

pineapple

apple

raspberries

lemon

mango

blueberries

strawberry

peach

plum

cherries

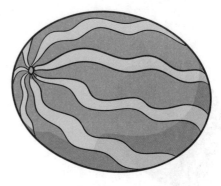

watermelon

Bite Into It

Circle the fruit whose skin you can't eat.

Find the Fruit

Find the fruit that makes a healthy snack!
Color the shapes with yellow dots.

Crunch and Munch

Some foods are crunchy when you bite into them.
Circle the foods that make a crunchy sound on both pages.

Fruit Colors

Which color matches each fruit?
Draw a line to connect the fruit to the right color splats. Then **color** the fruit.

apple

lemon

orange

grapes

watermelon

cherries

banana

kiwi

pineapple

Colorful Veggie Pairs

Draw a line to connect the vegetables that have matching colors.

Healthy Tic-Tac-Toe

Circle the healthy foods. Get three in a row to win!

Sports Match

Draw a line to connect each item to its matching sports equipment.

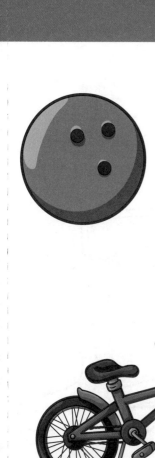

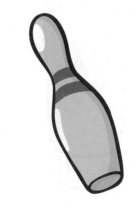

Clean Teeth

Circle the things you need for healthy teeth.

Squeaky Clean

Write the numbers **1**, **2**, and **3** to put the pictures
in the correct order for washing your hands.

Yoga Fun

Yoga is a good way to stretch your body.
Follow these pictures to **stretch** your muscles.

(1) "Sunrise"

(2)

"Airplane"

"Tree"

"Butterfly"

"Side Stretch"

To the Rescue

Draw a line to connect each first responder's equipment with their emergency vehicle.

School Ride

Connect the dots, from 1-8, to draw the missing bicycle wheel.

Dress Up

Circle the clothing that you might wear to a baseball game.
Choose a top, bottom, hat, and some shoes.

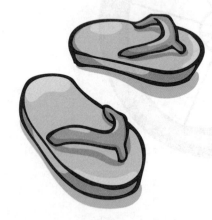
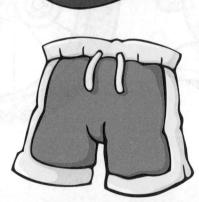

Dog Walk

Let's go to the park!
Write the numbers **1, 2,** and **3** to order the dog walking pictures.

Silly Sports

Let's play soccer!
Cross out the things these friends don't need to play their game.

Helmet Match

Draw a line to connect each helmet to its activity.

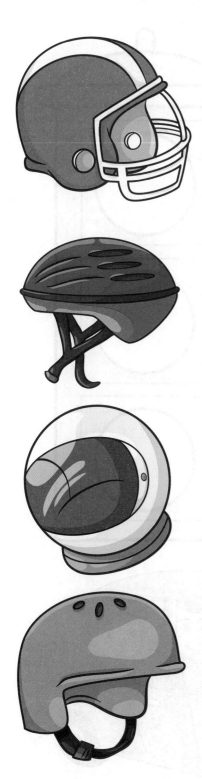

Traffic Lights

Red means stop, yellow means slow, green means go!
Trace the words and then **color** in the traffic lights to match the words.

stop

slow

go

Fork, Spoon, or Hands?

Food is eaten in many different ways. Under each kind of food,
circle the picture that shows how you eat it.

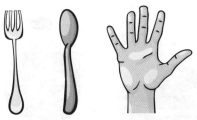

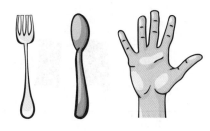

Food Around the World

Read and **trace** the country names below.
Then **draw** a line to match the food to the country it comes from.

sushi

croissant

apple pie

fish and chips

maple syrup

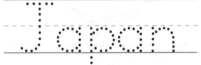

Japan

Canada

Britain

France

United States

What Will You Be?

Trace the name of each career below. What will you be?

artist

teacher

doctor

police

farmer

chef

Love Is All Around

Draw a picture for someone you love. **Write** their name and yours below.

To: _____

From: _____

Which Sense?

Match each kid to the sense they are pointing to.

smell

hear

taste

Favorite Sport

Draw a line between each character and the equipment they need for their activity.

baseball

ballet

skiing

soccer

hockey